ROLLS - ROYCE HER

ARMSTRONG SIDDELEY
—the Parkside story 1896–1939

Ray Cook

HISTORICAL SERIES No 11

Published in 1988 by the
Rolls-Royce Heritage Trust
PO Box 31 Derby England

©1988 Ray Cook

This book, or any parts thereof,
must not be reproduced in any form without the
written permission of the publisher

ISBN 0-9511710-3-8

The Historical Series is published as a joint initiative by the Rolls-Royce Heritage Trust and the Sir Henry Royce Memorial Foundation.

Also published in the series:
- No. 1 Rolls-Royce—the formative years, 1906–1939
  Alec Harvey-Bailey, published by RRHT
- No. 2 The Merlin in Perspective—the combat years
  Alec Harvey-Bailey, published by RRHT
- No. 3 Rolls-Royce—the pursuit of excellence
  Alec Harvey-Bailey and Mike Evans, published by HRMF
- No. 4 In the Beginning—The Manchester origins of Rolls-Royce
  Mike Evans, published by RRHT
- No. 5 Rolls-Royce—the Derby Bentleys
  Alec Harvey-Bailey, published by HRMF
- No. 6 The Early Days of Rolls-Royce—and the Montagu Family
  Lord Montagu of Beaulieu, published by RRHT
- No. 7 Rolls-Royce—Hives, the Quiet Tiger
  Alec Harvey-Bailey, published by HRMF
- No. 8 Rolls-Royce—Twenty to Wraith
  Alec Harvey-Bailey, published by HRMF
- No. 9 Rolls-Royce and the Mustang
  David Birch, published by RRHT
- No. 10 From Gipsy to Gem—with diversions
  Peter Stokes, published by RRHT

Cover: The Sphinx

Printed by Bemrose Security Printing, Derby

CONTENTS

		Page
1	Introduction	7
2	The Deasy Motor Car Company	12
3	The merger with Armstrong Whitworth	32
4	The Armstrong Siddeley Development Company	62
5	The formation of Hawker Siddeley Aircraft	108
Appendix I	The aero engines	128
Appendix II	Engines built for development or as prototypes	130
Appendix III	The cars	131
Appendix IV	Other Armstrong Siddeley designed engines	133
Appendix V	Genealogical table of Parkside Site to 1939	136
Appendix VI	Historical details of other companies connected with the story of Parkside	137

FOREWORD

The history of the Parkside site goes back to the turn of the century, and in those days it stood on the edge of a much smaller but highly industrialised city famous for its bicycles. The motor car was in its infancy but had already taken root in Coventry, and it was this that brought to Parkside one J.D. Siddeley. A gifted and versatile engineer, and a shrewd businessman, he soon stamped his personality on the company that was to become Armstrong Siddeley Motors. Cars were only one side of the business: in time the firm produced - with varying degrees of success - things as diverse as aero engines, cinema projectors, torpedo engines and railcars. Armstrong Siddeley engines might be found anywhere from the depths of the sea to the frontiers of space.

Today the name on the front of the factory is Rolls-Royce, as it is on others up and down the country which formerly bore other, no less famous ones. The traditions and the reputations of all these constituents contribute to the international standing of the present company, and it is right that their history be recorded while it is still relatively recent. The present book takes the story of Armstrong Siddeley Motors up to 1939, a time of change in more senses than one, and is written by one with the ideal background. Ray Cook began his career at Parkside in Armstrong Siddeley days and is an established historian, being a Member of Council and a vice-President of the Railway & Canal Historical Society.

To condense forty years of sometimes turbulent history into a few thousand words is no easy task, but all essential aspects are covered. Even one well versed in Armstrong Siddeley lore will find a few surprises in these pages. Illustrations play an important part in technical history, and the author has gone to some lengths in obtaining and preparing the best possible selection. This is the first contribution from our own Coventry Branch to a growing list of publications by the Rolls-Royce Heritage Trust. We have in Coventry a very active Branch whose premises are already well filled with historic machinery: another Parkside tradition in the making, perhaps?

D.W. RYALL C Eng., M I Prod.E, M B I M
Facility Manager, Parkside
October 1987

AUTHOR'S NOTES

In the course of compiling this work, the author has been acutely aware, not so much as to what is known, but what is not known, and in this area it is very apparent that the old Rolls-Royce company is far better served with archival material. How much of the older Parkside material was lost in the Coventry air-raids, or either dispersed or disposed of is unknown, but, as a practising railway historian, one is just as conscious of the frustration caused by the proverbial 'missing link'.

This has been very apparent even within the company Minute Books when, in one Board meeting, there are some technical details, and in another when the technical report of the Managing Director was read "it was resolved that the report be filed within the Minutes" - but none of these reports have, to date, come to light.

The frustration has extended not only to the lesser known products, but also to those better known. One example of this can be quoted with respect to the 45hp water-cooled engine in the Pavesi tractor. Was it a standard car engine; a modified one to cater for the more arduous conditions, or was it a totally new one? Equally so with the Siddeley built cinema projector. Despite the fact that the company Minutes refer to a company being set up in 1920, enquiries of several organisations, and the personal efforts of two well respected fellow railway historians, have failed totally to locate the company. One further example will suffice, and this concerns the well illustrated armoured car of around 1937, about which nothing is known. As David Fletcher of the Tank Museum observed "if it were a 1909 Latvian design there could be some excuse".

It is undoubtedly a fact that many of the old company drawings, especially the aero-engine ones, were destroyed in the air raids which gutted the aero drawing office over the canteen, but those remaining may reveal a little more about the unknown engines when collated against the drawing office registers.

The car side of the enterprise has all the appearance of being a veritable minefield, and in this respect is best left to the experts; the several members responsible for the individual car model registers within the Armstrong Siddeley Owners Club, and to Bill Smith, also of the Owners Club, whose knowledge of the company history extends well beyond the constraints of the company's cars. It is earnestly hoped that a definitive history of this aspect will emanate from this source. Would that the privately produced book *The Siddeley Collection* were still available.

Further frustration has arisen on the photographic side where all enquiries with respect to original Armstrong Whitworth aircraft photographs has come to naught, both in connection with the late Oliver Tapper's book on the company, and also those of Alan Campbell-Orde, for many years Armstrong Whitworth Aircraft's chief test pilot.

The information contained in the appendices has been compiled from the best available sources, confirmed, where possible, from the remaining company records. Any material which may augment, or correct, this information will be greatly appreciated.

Despite the many dead ends encountered, eventually, in the words of the recent religious exhortation - we will overcome!

September 1987

ACKNOWLEDGEMENTS

In compiling this comparatively short history the author is particularly indebted to the Coventry Branch Committee of the Rolls-Royce Heritage Trust for their help - both moral and financial - and their encouragement, in particular the Chairman, David Williams, and Ron Frost. Among the many individuals who have imparted information, especial thanks are due to George Day for his help on the aero engine and design aspects. Equally important contributors have been David Fletcher of the Tank Museum in unravelling the story of the company's involvement in tracked armoured vehicles; Bill Smith of the Armstrong Siddeley Owners Club for both information and for access to A.S.O.C. photographs; R.R. McCurrach and G. Foley, both ex-R.N. Submarines retired, for detailed information on the torpedo engines; Rodney Weaver for unearthing details of the Coventry railcar; David Rimmer, the Coventry City Archivist, for much early local information; Birmingham City Libraries, and finally to John Ellis, Brian Slatter and David Williams for checking the manuscript. Thanks are also extended to John Randle Siddeley, the present Lord Kenilworth, for his kindness in reading and commenting on the early pages of this work which refer to the family history of J.D. Siddeley, the first Baron.

Also gratefully acknowledged is the help of the many others, both individuals and organisations, who have contributed in part to this narrative.

As with all written works someone has the unenviable task of deciphering my scribble and I am indeed grateful to Marie Lapworth for handling this most ably. Finally, to my wife who has had to cope with an untidy house during its compilation, and also the inconvenience of a bathroom darkroom.

Amongst the photographic acknowledgements, those of the Imperial War Museum are reproduced with the permission of the Trustees of the Imperial War Museum, London, whilst the abbreviation A.S.O.C. is used for those of the Armstrong Siddeley Owners Club. Thanks are also extended to the Royal Air Force Museum, the Tank Museum, British Aerospace plc, R.A. Clarke, Gordon Coltas, Military Aircraft Photographs (MAP), Les Neil, Peter Whitehead and Paul Marshall for permission to use photographs from their collections. One final acknowledgement needs to be made: to Alan Cheeseman, who has almost repaired the act of vandalism which resulted in so many of the company negatives being 'disposed of' several years ago.

September 1987

Chapter 1
INTRODUCTION

The name Armstrong Siddeley first appeared in 1919. Its emergence was the product of a merger between the Siddeley-Deasy Motor Car Company and the much larger shipbuilding and engineering concern of Sir W.G. Armstrong Whitworth based at Newcastle-upon-Tyne.

The driving force behind the merger was John Davenport Siddeley, whose earliest engineering business can be traced to the last decade of the 19th century. J.D. Siddeley was born at Longsight, in Manchester, in August 1866, the son of William Siddeley of Altrincham. The family name can be traced back to Rondle Siddeley, who died in 1621 and whose son's name, Randle, is perpetuated in that of the present Lord Kenilworth.

John Siddeley was a champion cyclist for the Humber Cycle Company in his younger days, and in 1892 he joined that company and became its only designer draughtsman. However, he was not destined to stay there long because his organising ability – possibly in connection with cycling – had come to the attention of Harvey du Cros, the owner of the Dunlop patents, and Managing Director of the Pneumatic Tyre Company, which became the Dunlop Tyre Company in 1898. Du Cros offered Siddeley a post in his Belfast factory, and in March 1893 he left for Ireland, pausing in Manchester long enough to marry Sarah Goodier. He remained in Ireland until after the birth of their first child, Cyril, in August 1894, and returned to England as a representative of the company.

By 1898 he had acquired sufficient confidence and knowledge of the pneumatic tyre to set up the Clipper Tyre Company in Fleet Street, which was the continuation of Smithford Street, Coventry, and, to prove the quality of his product, he undertook the arduous cycle ride from Lands End to John O'Groats. The Dunlop Company could hardly have been pleased when his company moved to Alma Street in 1901, just along the road from the Dunlop factory and next door to their fire engine house.

Even before the end of the century his interest was shifting from tyres to the motor vehicles using them, and he became an avid motorist. In 1900 he entered two 6hp Parisien Daimler cars in the 1000 mile Reliability Trials organised by the Royal Automobile Club, one of which he drove himself, fitted with his own Clipper tyres. Amongst other objectives, the trial was to test the tyres and not the cars but, in the event, both cars were amongst the twenty four finishers, one of them achieving sixth place.

In 1901 he resigned as Managing Director of the Clipper Company, which was taken over by Dunlop shortly afterwards, and became the British importer of Peugeot cars. This was largely to gain experience of the rapidly developing car industry, and, early in 1902, he formed the Siddeley Autocar Company based in Garfield Road in Coventry, next door to the Rover factory. The first Siddeley car was merely a thinly disguised Peugeot, with both chassis and engine being imported, although the body was locally

John Siddeley's first Coventry venture was the formation, in Fleet Street, of the Clipper Tyre Company. Shortly after moving to Alma Street in 1901 he resigned and formed the Siddeley Autocar Company. This c1908 shot of the Alma Street premises, although still displaying the original name, was now part of Dunlop. (*from a postcard courtesy Les Neil*)

made. At the old Crystal Palace Motor Show early in 1903, four models were on display ranging from a single cylinder 6hp to a four cylinder 18/24hp. It was not long, however, before John Siddeley decided that his name should appear on a wholly British made car, and in company with Lionel de Rothschild, whom he knew well, he approached the well known engineering company of Vickers Sons and Maxim at Crayford, in Kent, to design and build a car to his own specifications which would feature a vertical engine rather than the still very popular horizontal one. This was carried out in 1903 by the Wolseley Tool and Motor Car Company, which had been set up by Vickers in 1901 to take over the car manufacturing side of the Wolseley Sheep-Shearing Machine Company, one of the oldest car manufacturers in the country. The cars were made at Crayford and were very well received, and Vickers became very impressed with Siddeley, especially with his advanced ideas on engines, the use of aluminium, and also the development of propeller shaft drive for the smaller cars in lieu of the more common and heavier chain drive.

The cars were sold from an office in York Street, Westminster, almost opposite those of the Wolseley company and, following prompting by the parent Board, the company approached John Siddeley with a view to taking over his business entirely. This was achieved early in 1905 with Siddeley becoming their Sales Manager and, from then until 1910, a range of cars with vertical engines were marketed as Wolseley-Siddeley

THE LITTLE SIDDELEY CAR
SIDDELEY AUTOCAR CO
1903

and were very successful as a marque. A range of buses were produced from 1906 to 1909 under the same name.

However, there was a cloud on the horizon in the form of Wolseley's Manager and Chief Designer, Herbert Austin, who had been manager of the Wolseley Sheep Shearing Machine Company since 1892, and had moved to the car company when it was formed.

Austin was a trained engineer and strongly favoured the horizontal engine, using motor racing to promote the company's products, while Siddeley, who was more the intuitive designer, took the opposite standpoint with his own vertical engines and active participation in reliability trials as the basis for promotion. It soon became apparent that these two strong minded characters could not agree to differ for very long. The feud resulted in many contentious arguments, until eventually a 'contest' was arranged between the two types of engine. Relations between Austin and Siddeley were strained from the moment the engines were started up – and rapidly deteriorated! Unfortunately, it was Siddeley's engine which broke down first and there were veiled hints of sabotage, although these can be attributed more to pique than to fact. Austin had won this round, but a single test of this nature could hardly have been conclusive in proving one or the

Carriage Work.

Siddeley autocars carried in stock are fitted with tonneau bodies. Any type of body illustrated in the following designs can be supplied to order. Prices on application.

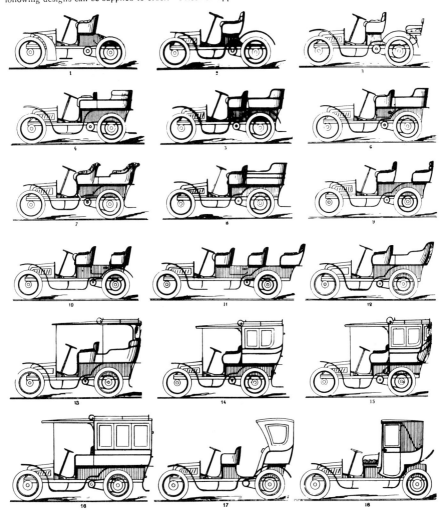

SIDDELEY AUTOCAR CO.

Early body option advertisement.

other. Austin's adherence to the horizontal engine eventually led to disagreements with the Wolseley Board and he resigned in 1905, going on to found the Austin works at Longbridge in 1906, leaving John Siddeley to take over the post of General Manager.

In private hands and beautifully restored, this 1904 model – now known as Green Goddess – is one of the earliest genuine Siddeley cars. Despite being manufactured by Wolseley, and assembled by Vickers at Crayford for the Siddeley Autocar Co., it is powered by a 12hp twin-cylinder engine designed by John Siddeley. (*Author*).

Siddeley's faith in the vertical engine was to be more than vindicated, but many years later his rigid attitude towards engine design was to prove less successful. He remained with the Wolseley company until 1909 when he left to join the Deasy concern.

Chapter 2
THE DEASY MOTOR CAR COMPANY

The Deasy Motor Car Manufacturing Company was founded in February 1906, under the sponsorship of Captain H.H.P. Deasy, to manufacture cars to the design of E.W. Lewis. Deasy, an ex-cavalryman, had fixed ideas on the type of car which was to carry his name. Lewis was recruited from the Rover company, which was building both engines and chassis' in a factory in Rover Road, Coventry, to become Works Manager, Chief Designer and Engineer. He was described as being a 'determined and truculent' character with his own firm ideas, and it was not long before the two clashed on design questions.

Henry Hugh Peter Deasy had been born in Dublin in 1866, the son of the Right Honourable Rickard Deasy, Lord Justice of Appeal in Ireland. He joined the Army in 1888 and, upon his retirement in 1897, his talents as a surveyor were used to good effect in Tibet and China over a three year exploration. For this work he received the Royal Geographical Society's Gold Medal in 1900. His interest in cars appears to date from about 1903, in which year he drove a Rochet-Schneider car from London to

The Parkside frontage of the Iden Motor Company c1905 seen from Short Street. The building dated 1897 is still extant but now has a new built-on brick facade, but is still recognisable.

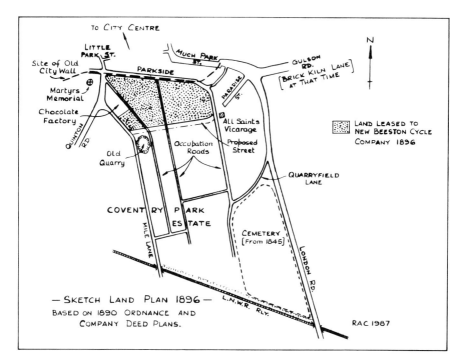

Glasgow without a stop, and later drove a Martini car along the trackbed of the mountain rack-railway from the outskirts of Montreux, in Switzerland, to the summit at Rochers-de-Naye. Deasy already had a company of his own, H.H.P. Deasy and Company. At that time it had control of the Swiss Martini company, and was still in existence when the new company was founded, importing both Martini and Rochet-Schneider cars. The first meeting of the new company took place on 20 February 1906 at the North Western Hotel in Liverpool, at which the financial accounts of Deasy's company were presented. It was resolved that the new company should be filed with the Registrar of Joint Stock Companies on the next day with a share capital of £80,000 in £1 shares. The company was to negotiate the lease of the defunct Iden Motor Company factory in Parkside from the liquidators for the sum of £12,820. On 12 March, Deasy was appointed Chairman of the company, which had its sales and administration housed at Brompton Road in London. The Directors approved two recommendations on 20 March: the first was to approve the payment of £12,179 on completion of the leasehold agreement with the receiver of the Iden Company, the Deasy Company already having paid £641, the second was that Mr. Lewis be authorised to negotiate contracts for the supply of materials sufficient to build 100 cars.

The land involved in this transaction totalled just over 7 acres, and had originally been leased by William Meriton, Lord Cheylesmore, to the New Beeston Cycle Company from 21 December 1896 for a period of 99 years and, over the following years, the land was the subject of many changes and leases. The border of the land ran along the whole frontage on the south side of Parkside through to Quinton Road, whilst the southern boundary ran approximately parallel to Parkside from roughly the north side of No.2

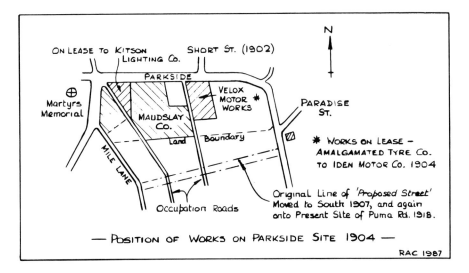

— Position of Works on Parkside Site 1904 —

RAC 1987

gate through to Mile Lane, where to the south it bordered on an old quarry. The only part of the block not contained in the lease was a triangle of land from Mile Lane to the small occupation road still to be seen on the corner almost opposite the Martyr's Memorial, the southern boundary of which was approximately opposite the old Cheylesmore school. This triangle was already in the hands of J.P. Rademacher who ran a chocolate factory there. In view of later connections with the Maudslay company in the First World War, it is opportune to mention that, in 1902, Maudslay acquired a large portion of the central area from the occupation road through to Parkside for their car factory, and which they only vacated in 1953. The Deasy company, in fact, used only the portion from a further occupation road, almost opposite to Short Street, around to No.2 gate, and a strip at the rear of the Maudslay factory.

The final transfer of the property took place on 2 April 1906, the Company's seal being affixed, and on 10 April it was resolved that the manufacturing side of the business should be separated from the design. The appointment of W.G. Williams to the post of Works Manager was proposed and confirmed shortly afterwards, with Lewis as General Manager. Williams had previously been the manager of the Collier Tyre Company.

In May 1906, £700 was authorised for the procurement of equipment for making car bodies on a limited scale, with an announcement to be made that the company would undertake repairs of any make of car. The first car to leave the works appears to have been a 15hp model completed towards the end of that month although, at the first statutory Annual General Meeting on 28 May, it was stated that initial production would be a 24hp model selling at £500 complete. Where the initial batch of parts for the cars came from is somewhat obscure, because an area for body building was only just being contemplated, and Deasy and Williams had been authorised to visit Paris for the purpose of considering the purchase of bodies from France. It is almost certain that Deasy used his connections with the Martini company to enable production to begin.

To participate in the Motor Show at Olympia in November 1906, the company rented 800 square feet of space for £40, and also paid £10 to become a member of the Society of Motor Manufacturers and Traders. Three cars and a chassis were exhibited and the company paid for all employees to travel down to the show. However, even at this early stage, there was dissatisfaction between Captain Deasy and the Parkside works because no car was available for demonstration at the opening of the show. From the ensuing correspondence, it appears that Deasy was an infrequent visitor to the works, even though in October it had been resolved that two of the Directors should visit the factory at least once a month. That he had cause for complaint is without question, some of the delay resulting from Lewis's advanced ideas, and some from the lack of manufacturing experience.

A demonstration car finally arrived for the last two days of the show, after being returned to Parkside earlier in the week to eliminate excessive bevel noise from the back axle. Following the show, another car was taken to London and this too was returned with complaints of defective steering and wheel wobble, whilst two cars entered for the 1906 Tourist Trophy Race both suffered crankshaft failure – one before even reaching the starting line, and the other before completing a lap. Both drivers were injured and, although it is unrecorded, one was possibly fatal. In December a donation of ten guineas was authorised to a hospital in the Isle of Man, in recognition of their services.

The flow of adverse criticism from Deasy continued through the rest of the year and into 1907. His report to the Board meeting in December with respect to the car supplied for test reads like a motoring disaster: steering defective, wheel wobble, defective clutch, gear change lever plate broken, reverse gear difficult to engage, no mesh in first gear, gear box noise, car did not move when clutch let in, defective footbrake. Finally the car was sent back by train! It is difficult to understand how a car in this condition was allowed out of the works, but worse was to follow. In January 1907, a glowing report was submitted to Lewis by Williams with respect to a car he had tested under difficult conditions in Derbyshire, but in February, Deasy's faith in Lewis and the company was finally shattered on a 1,500 mile business trip to Biarritz in France and back. During the trip the left-hand axle bracket broke, the car lost a wheel, and ended up in a French ditch but, after receiving new parts, he completed his journey, arriving back with a list of complaints running to almost two pages. The rift opening up between Deasy and Lewis became wider after Deasy relinquished his position as Managing Director, although he retained his Ordinary Directorship.

The conflict between the two finally came to a head in February 1908, after the Board resolved to enter a 25hp and a 35hp car in the two major reliability trials of that year, despite Deasy's objections to one of the cars being driven by a Mr. Graham, and the whole organisation being in Lewis's hands. It was decided that the resolution should stand. Whatever the reasons for Deasy's objections, they appear to have been unjustified. The car driven by George Mason, later head of the Road Test Department, won a Gold Mèdal in the arduous Scottish Reliability Trial, whilst that driven by Graham took second place in the 2000 mile Royal Automobile Club Trial, behind a car of far greater power and cost, with the second Deasy car in third place.

A fortnight later, Deasy decided he could no longer tolerate the situation and resigned on 9 March 1908. However, Lewis did not win the battle because the Board meeting on 15 April, at which Deasy's resignation was accepted, also resolved that Lewis should vacate the works and become consulting engineer to the company on a full-time basis, subject to all designs and other changes being approved by the Managing Director. H.A. Smith became the new Works Manager and, although the company at this time was in a somewhat perilous position, sufficient of the small number of cars produced were sold – despite Deasy's complaints – to ensure further orders. Under the new

MERITORIOUS PERFORMANCE
OF A 24-H.P.
DEASY
OVER ROUGH IRISH ROADS.

1905

"Captain Deasy has completed his thousand miles Reliability Trial in Ireland WITHOUT A SINGLE INVOLUNTARY STOP. Made complete circuit of country. Experienced very bad weather throughout, and covered some of roughest roads in Ireland. Car behaved splendid throughout, not requiring a single adjustment from start to finish. Dunlop Tyres stood splendidly, and did not require pumping once." — T. W. MURPHY, Official Observer on behalf of Irish Automobile Club.

PRICE LISTS AND FULL PARTICULARS POST FREE.

THE DEASY MOTOR CAR MFG. CO., Ltd.,
10, Brompton Road, London, S.W.

Telegrams:
"Deasy, London."

Telephone:
1144 and 3082 Western.

Works:
COVENTRY.

The Deasy company's fitting shop in 1910.

manager, reliability improved to the extent that, by the end of 1908, the reputation of the company had been enhanced considerably.

E.W. Lewis remained with the company under the new regime, his contract with the company extending until at least 1915, and, although the butt of Captain Deasy's comments, his ideas were, unfortunately, in advance of the technology of the day. The later widespread use of his ideas for transverse springing and aluminium back axle casings were but two examples. Prior to his departure, Deasy had visions of his company becoming considerably larger and, with this in mind, the company negotiated a further lease from Lord Cheylesmore on 12 September 1907 for the tract of land between Mile Lane and Parkside from the original boundary to a new "proposed street" closer to what later became Puma Road.

John Siddeley, meanwhile, was having problems of his own with the Vickers management, and, hearing of Deasy's resignation, and Lewis's misfortunes, he applied for the post of General Manager of the company early in 1909. Having been appointed, he left the Wolseley company and moved up to Coventry, but he was not to remain in that position for long. On 24 June the Board approved his appointment as Managing Director with a seat on the Board. This appointment became both a salvation for the ailing Parkside works and the basis for the company's later success. One of his first decisions was to transfer the administration from London to Parkside, leaving the former purely as a sales outlet and showroom. In June the company dispensed entirely with Williams' services, Williams having earlier moved from Parkside to Brompton Road as Commercial Manager. It was also agreed to dispose of the body building, which was reported by Siddeley in 1910 as having made a considerable loss. Over the

1910 JDS-Type Deasy Landaulette.

next twelve months the production facilities were completely reorganised and the range of cars redesigned.

The new range became known as the "J.D.S. Type Deasy" in 1910, although production continued through the year on two of the old Deasy designs. The first cars to carry the new name were 14/20hp and 18/28hp models which featured pair-cast cylinders for their 4 cylinder engines, with thermo-syphon cooling, and these were shortly followed by a 12hp 2 litre car. Chassis prices for the larger car started at £365. An outstanding feature of the cars was the large coffinlike bonnet – an expression John Siddeley thought abhorrent – and bulkhead mounted radiator. Production at that time was normally six per week, and when the 12hp was introduced it was decided to buy the chassis from the Rover Company and the engine from Asters, the bodies being supplied from various other companies. In fact, apart from the radiators, Parkside became merely an assembly and testing facility.

By 1911, only the "J.D. Siddeley-Type Deasy" cars, as they were now called, were advertised, but at this point a complication arose for the company. Even before Herbert Austin left Wolseley, a range of cars with Siddeley's vertical engine was being marketed as Wolseley-Siddeley, although they were often sold as Siddeley or even Vickers. They continued to be produced until 1910, by which time the Siddeley side of the business had been officially transferred to the Deasy concern. By early 1911, the Wolseley company began to bombard the company with letters concerning the use of the name 'Siddeley', and the matter was placed in the hands of the company's solicitors. The

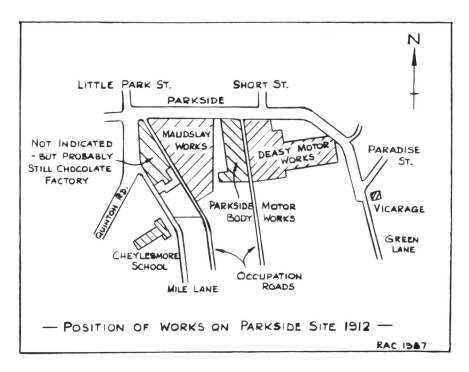

— Position of Works on Parkside Site 1912 —

correspondence went on beyond the middle of the year, but the outcome is not recorded in the Minutes. However, the Wolseley-Siddeley marque name disappeared late in 1910.

Although plans were already being drawn up to enter the commercial vehicle market, it was resolved that they should not be pursued as it was "likely to prejudice the name of the company as makers of high class cars".

All the first cars of the new regime were powered by poppet valve engines – from Asters for the 12hp, and from Daimler for the larger ones. However, in 1911 the company began negotiations with Daimler for the supply of the Knight double sleeve valve engines, not only for the 4 cylinder cars, but also for a new 6 cylinder model which was being planned. An agreement was made in the early part of 1912 and, by the following year, all cars were fitted with this type of engine. The Knight engines were very quiet running, but such was Siddeley's quest for improvement, that each engine was stripped down on delivery and the sleeves carefully checked and, if necessary, machined and polished to give reduced friction, and improved inlet and exhaust flow patterns. An enthusiastic journalist wrote of the cars that they were "as silent and inscrutable as the Sphinx". This phrase appealed greatly to John Siddeley and, shortly after, he decided that the Grecian version of this Egyptian monument, in the sitting position and in male form, should be the company's emblem and the details were sent to Moles at Birmingham for the castings to be made for the radiator caps. It also appeared as a logo on the company's advertisements, but was not registered as an emblem, or trade mark, until late in 1920.

The problem with the Wolseley company over the use of the name 'Siddeley' was eventually resolved, and in 1912 the cars became advertised as the J.D. Siddeley-Type

Siddeley-Deasy Advertisement for 1913. (*Bill Smith*)

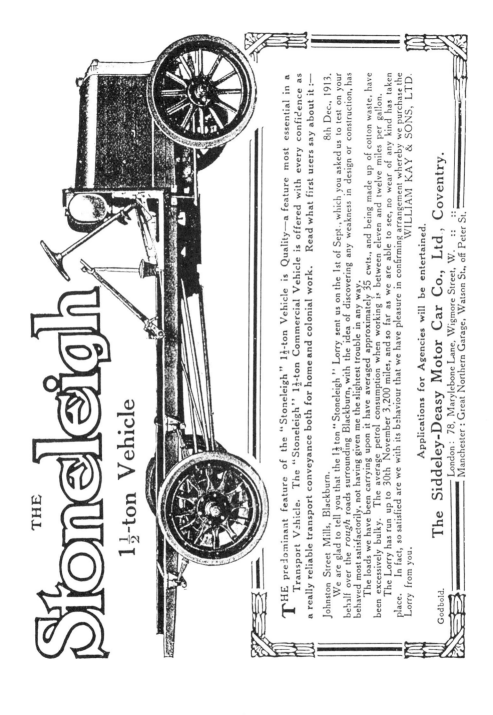

THE Stoneleigh
1½-ton Vehicle

Johnston Street Mills, Blackburn.
8th Dec., 1913.

THE predominant feature of the "Stoneleigh" 1½-ton Vehicle is Quality—a feature most essential in a Transport Vehicle. The "Stoneleigh" 1½-ton Commercial Vehicle is offered with every confidence as a really reliable transport conveyance both for home and colonial work. Read what first users say about it :—

We are glad to tell you that the 1½-ton "Stoneleigh" Lorry sent us on the 1st of Sept., which you asked us to test on your behalf over the *rough* roads surrounding Blackburn, with the idea of discovering any weakness in design or construction, has behaved most satisfactorily, not having given me the slightest trouble in any way.

The loads we have been carrying upon it have averaged approximately 35 cwts., and being made up of cotton waste, have been excessively bulky. The average petrol consumption when working is between eleven and twelve miles per gallon.

The Lorry has run up to 30th November 3,200 miles, and so far as we are able to see, no wear of any kind has taken place. In fact, so satisfied are we with its behaviour that we have pleasure in confirming arrangement whereby we purchase the Lorry from you.

WILLIAM KAY & SONS, LTD.

Godbold.

Applications for Agencies will be entertained.

The Siddeley-Deasy Motor Car Co., Ltd., Coventry.

London : 78, Marylebone Lane, Wigmore Street, W. :: ::
Manchester : Great Northern Garage, Watson St., off Peter St.

Deasy. The big 6 cylinder Knight engined 24/30hp was introduced in the same year, whilst the company obtained valuable publicity as a result of a Royal Automobile Club observed 15,000 mile reliability trial, run almost entirely on the Brooklands racing circuit. One can feel somewhat sorry for the drivers on a trial of this nature, which took over two months to complete with a regular 300 miles continuous driving per day, apart from Sundays and holidays. The car involved was a 14/20hp model and it was reported that there were no involuntary stops during the tests, only £2 being spent on new parts. The overall average speed is recorded as being marginally under 35mph.

Two further events of note occurred in 1912; the first of these being the formation of Stoneleigh Motors Limited to handle the light car market and, eventually, commercial vehicles, for which sanction for three sample vehicles had already been approved. The second event showed clearly the control Siddeley now had over the company, when an Extraordinary General Meeting on 7 November unanimously voted to change the company's name to Siddeley-Deasy Motor Car Company. For 1913 the entire car range was powered by Knight sleeve-valve engines, but in February John Siddeley suggested to the Board that the company should manufacture its own engines. This was agreed, and the necessary funds were allocated to purchase the machine tools, and also for the expansion of the premises. This decision was to prove crucial to the company's prosperity following the events at Sarajevo, and the subsequent declaration of war with Germany in August 1914.

In July 1913 negotiations had begun for the company to acquire the goodwill of the London based Burlington Carriage Company, in order that all car body production could be controlled from Parkside, by employing a good coachbuilding concern to manufacture Burlington bodies to be shipped to Parkside.

A month earlier, the first small commercial vehicle had been test run successfully and a small batch was to be put in hand. However, prior to the declaration of war only two had been produced. The first Stoneleigh car had already been produced by that time, and was, in fact, almost a copy of the Daimler built B.S.A. light car with a 13.9hp Knight sleeve-valve engine. Advertisements of the period indicate that the vehicle was probably Daimler built, with a front radiator and redesigned bonnet.

While all these developments were going on, the prosperous, and peaceful years of the early 20th century were drawing rapidly to a close. When war was declared on 4 August 1914, the slogan 'business as usual' did not apply to normal industrial work, and John Siddeley prepared for the closure of the works and expressed his desire that all single able-bodied men should join the forces. As production was run down, the younger elements amongst the workforce gradually went to war, little realising the vital importance of mechanisation in the coming conflict, both on land and in the air. Suddenly, out of the blue, an order arrived for 100 Stoneleigh lorries for Russia, to be fitted out as ambulances and field kitchens. It was a turning point for the company, and no doubt a problem for the management with so many of the workforce having departed. As a consequence, many of them received telegrams requesting them to return to the plant. The delivery date of the order was fairly tight and tested the Parkside capacity to the limit, a working week of 95 to 110 hours being not uncommon, and in order to increase output a nightshift was started. This, however, was not the first war work which had come Parkside's way, as for some time the War Office had been buying the 18hp model for use both as staff cars and in ambulance form, the vehicles being subject to stringent tests on the flat, and on hill climbs, before final acceptance.

Two further events of note occurred during 1914. In June the indentures of the first three apprentices to be taken on by the company were signed, and F.R. Smith arrived

A line-up of 26 18hp Siddeley-Deasy ambulances destined for France with the 1st Convoy B.E.F. The one extreme right is a Calcutta War Gift.

from Aberdonia Cars in London to become Chief Designer. The picture painted of him is that he was somewhat eccentric in character, and rather absent-minded, but his design and development work for the company was to prove of inestimable value.

The Russian order began the surge of war production from the plant; more lorries for Russia, which entailed a hurriedly arranged trip by one of the engineers in order to tune the engines to suit the harsh climate in northern Russia; 18hp chassis for ambulances, built both at Parkside and at Calcott Brothers factory in Far Gosford Street, Coventry; collaboration with the Standard Motor Company who were contracted to supply parts for the ambulances; sub-contract work for Maudslay commercial vehicles and, of course, 18hp cars for the War Office.

At the Board meeting in January 1915, John Siddeley made a recommendation that was to change totally the business outlook of the company. After careful consideration, the Board authorised him to enter into contracts to extend the plant in order to build aircraft, and also to tender for associated Government contracts. At the same meeting, A.G. Asbury, who had joined the company from the Wolseley company in 1909, was appointed Works Manager, having previously been Works Superintendent and, as the war dragged on, he was to play a major part in organising the production facilities.

At the beginning of the war, flying was really in its infancy, being more for sporting personalities than for His Majesty's forces. However, by mid-1915 it was realised, principally, at that time, by the Navy, that these primitive machines had a part to play in the war effort. With expansion of the plant proceeding apace, Siddeley-Deasy became one of half a dozen companies chosen to manufacture both aircraft and engines. Even though one of the smallest, the organisation and ability of John Siddeley and his team was considered good enough to carry out the work. Siddeley had some experience of

John Siddeley's 1915 18hp Siddeley-Deasy tourer. In the rear are his wife, Sarah, and their daughters, Joan and Nancy. The driver is Ernest Siddeley. Alongside him is, possibly, the youngest son, Norman. Note the absence of the Sphinx mascot. (*courtesy of the Siddeley family*)

aircraft engines from his days at Wolseley, who were amongst the pioneers of the industry. This early work eventually culminated in an anglicised version of the Hispano V8 engine which emerged as the well known Wolseley Viper. The company had, however, nothing to offer in the way of experience in aircraft construction, but there was little such experience within industry generally.

The first contract for aircraft engines came in June 1915 for 300 at the rate of 10 per week, plus spares, which became equivalent to $12\frac{1}{2}$ per week. A letter from John Siddeley in the Company Minute Books refers to this being for 12 cylinder engines and an agreed total price of £300,000, which was considerably more than the company's normal turnover in such a short period. The letter also records a War Office contract for a large number of ambulances. Despite the reference to the 12 cylinder engines, the first engines turned out by the company were the 8 cylinder R.A.F. 1a, designed by the Royal Aircraft Factory at Farnborough. This 90hp V8 air-cooled engine, based on the Renault V8, was soon found to be both unreliable and underpowered, and only 25 were built before it was superseded by the 150hp 90° V12 air-cooled R.A.F. 4a engine referred to in the Siddeley letter. F.R. Smith was blooded on this engine, which required a certain amount of redesign in order to improve its reliability. The aircraft powered by this engine were the RE.7, RE.8 and BE.12.

Late in 1915, plans were being made for a housing scheme close to the plant to house the ever-expanding workforce, but it was to be a further two years before this came to fruition, despite the fact that a further order for 650 engines had been promised. Even with arrangements as they were, the first batch of ambulances had been delivered by October 1915. One consequence of the increased production was the appointment of A.J. Austen to the new post of Chief Accountant, which was a necessary step due to the increased turnover.The flood of orders continued into 1916, forcing the company to expand right up to the "proposed street" at the boundary of their lease. They were also forced to rent additional premises and to sub-contract portions of the work. By mid-1916 the orders for engines were up to 30 a week plus spares, and plans for future expansion were being made, and also the provision of a canteen for the considerable numbers of staff being recruited.

Towards the end of 1916, the company was asked to switch production to the new 6 cylinder in-line water-cooled B.H.P. (Beardmore-Halford-Pullinger) engine designed by Capt. (later Major) Frank Halford in collaboration with Beardmores, the Scottish Engineering and Shipbuilding company, and T.C. Pullinger, the Managing Director of Arrol Johnson. The Galloway Engine Company was set up by Pullinger to develop the engine, and the promise of the prototypes was such that large numbers were ordered by the War Office, but Galloway's were unable to satisfy the demand and the contract was offered to Parkside. Although designed to produce in the region of 300hp, this proved to be rather optimistic and it ultimately produced only 240hp.

John Siddeley accepted the offer, provided that one of the few engines already built could be tested at Parkside. One duly arrived, but proved to be unreliable, and also unsatisfactory in many other respects. Redesign was carried out by F.R. Smith, together with a newcomer to the company, Capt. (later Major) F.M. Green, of whom more in due course, and this involved a completely new aluminium cylinder head and water jacket in place of the original cast-iron head and sheet steel water jackets. Under Siddeley's direction, screwed-in open-ended cylinders were substituted for the existing closed-end ones, a feature which was later to prove an inspired one. There were, however, considerable delays with the contract, and it was not finally signed until late in 1917. In the meantime the company received further contracts for more R.A.F. 4a engines, and the RE.8 aircraft which were powered by them.

The building of aircraft at Parkside dates back to the early part of 1916 with an order for the RE.7 light reconnaissance and bomber aircraft. 100 of these were produced before production switched to the newly designed RE.8, which was a far more advanced aircraft powered by the R.A.F. 4a. This involved more expansion of the plant due to the quantity and delivery rate required. Having rented the body shop of the adjoining Swift Motor Company, part of which is now the Coventry Climax site on the east side of Mile Lane, negotiations were begun for more land from the Cheylesmore estate. The first two aircraft built were taken in sections to Farnborough by road for flight testing, but subsequent production aircraft were flown direct from Radford aerodrome, towards the north side of the city, the site of which is now part of the Daimler works belonging to Jaguar Cars. Over 1,000 RE.8s were produced before the armistice, which were powered by both Siddeley built engines, and ones from other contractors. Almost at the end of the war an order was received for 150 DH.10a aircraft, but only some half dozen were in course of erection, and when the contract was cancelled these were broken up. As a matter of interest the company also produced over 1,000 aircraft propellers during the war.

The first Siddeley aero engine was the 18.8 litre Puma, a redesigned production version of the 6 cylinder water-cooled BHP/Galloway Adriatic. It eventually produced 240hp, and 310hp in a high compression version in 1918 which did not go into production.

The problem of further expansion was resolved in 1917 with the acquisition of the portion of land through to the railway, including a repositioned "proposed street", later to become Puma Road, the south side of which became known as the Burlington Works. As recounted earlier, the Burlington Carriage Company had been acquired in August 1913 and set up as a subsidiary company with a nominal share capital of £5,000, all to be held by nominees of Siddeley-Deasy, to build Burlington car bodies for the company. There being no suitable site near the Burlington Company's offices in Marylebone Road, London, it was decided to set up the company in Coventry using

R.E.8 aircraft on assembly in the Burlington works 1918.

their offices here at the Charlesworth Bodies Works in Much Park Street, where some Burlington bodies were already being made. It is doubtful if this was ever arranged with the outbreak of war being imminent, and the company was finally set up within the Parkside complex. Other land was acquired, including more from Lord Cheylesmore, between Parkside and the London Road, though this contained provisions for the improvement of Parkside. The housing scheme finally got under way, following the purchase by the Ministry of land on the opposite side of the London Road from a prominent local landowner, Col. Wyley. Tenders were invited for building all the houses on the roads leading off Acacia Avenue as far down as the River Sherbourne, and for those fronting London Road. Finally, the old Vicarage of All Saints at the top of Paradise Street was converted into what is now the Sphinx Social Club, although the physical move from within the works did not take place until 1926.

To return to 1916 and to Capt. Green, whose name has already been mentioned, and the circumstances under which he joined the company. There had been complaints in Parliament during that year alleging inefficiency at the Royal Aircraft Factory at Farnborough and, as a result, a Committee of Inquiry was set up. When its findings were reported in 1917, it recommended that the design and construction of aircraft and engines at the factory should be terminated and be transferred into private companies. This was a drastic move in the middle of a world war, but the government endorsed the report and many highly skilled personnel left the factory. In many ways it was fortuitous for Siddeley-Deasy who recruited three of them; these were Green, who became Chief Engineer, John Lloyd, head of the Stress Department, who became head of the aircraft team, and S.D. Heron, an engine designer, whose speciality was cylinder

Puma crankcases in production in the top machine shop in 1918.

design. Capt. Green had been in charge of engine design at Farnborough since 1910 and, before coming to Parkside, he obtained permission to bring the preliminary designs of the projected R.A.F.8 14 cylinder 22.4 litre air-cooled radial engine.

However, with money advanced by the Ministry, work on the B.H.P. engine had already begun, the task of redesign having been completed early in 1917 and, as both Smith and Green were fully engaged in bringing the engine into production, the radial engine project was deferred. The redesigned B.H.P. was originally called the Siddeley 1S, but shortly afterwards was renamed the Puma, becoming the first aero engine to carry the company's name. The rapid expansion of the factory kept pace with the rise in output, although initially the new engine was beset by problems with the use of aluminium – a material whose properties were only just beginning to be understood, both in use and in manufacture. However, by the end of the war, it had become a thoroughly reliable unit to the extent that the company was producing 600 per month, peaking in the last few months of the war to 160 per week. Total production was some 6,000, mainly for the de Havilland DH.9 bomber aircraft and, ultimately, more were produced than any other engine in the country at that time.

During the work on the Puma, one of the subcontractors to Parkside was the Sir W.G. Armstrong Whitworth Company in Newcastle who, initially, supplied cylinder head castings and, later, the complete machined head. It is also probable that they produced some of the connecting rods. John Siddeley was very impressed with the quality of their products and the sub-contracting continued into the peacetime built engines. This was the first link with the concern which was to play such an important part in the later fortunes of the company.

Even before the end of the war, John Siddeley had been considering the peacetime market potentials and, in particular, the possible effect on company car design and production. His business acumen was such that, during the early part of 1918, he secretly imported an American $5\frac{1}{2}$ litre Marmon car, through the British Delco agents, to study how their technology had advanced in the three year period before they became directly involved in the war – in fact, their involvement stimulated rather than retarded progress. Widespread machine production had been adopted in their car industry, and their methods were now far ahead of our own and would threaten many previously secure British markets. During the final few months of the war it became possible to divert some of the design staff away from the war effort to concentrate on the design of the post war cars. John Siddeley had recently acquired Crackley Hall, now St. Joseph's Convent School, near Kenilworth, having previously lived at Hill Orchard at Meriden. It was at Crackley Hall that a small team was brought together in his billiard room where they were able to work in considerable secrecy. His foresight resulted in Siddeley-Deasy becoming the first company to introduce a new car after the war had ended.

Before recounting the events of the two years following the war, which involved the complete restructuring of the company, there was a comparatively minor event which reflected the company's attention to detail. This occurred in the early months of 1919 with the discovery of a man, apparently lost, wandering around the car assembly area. On enquiry it transpired that he was F. Gordon Crosby, a famous professional artist, who had travelled up from London at the behest of John Siddeley, whom he knew well, to look at the shape of the front end of the new car, which no-one seemed able to make aesthetically acceptable. He was shown the mock-up of the new car's bonnet and radiator, and proceeded to sketch the outline as it stood. He wandered off and returned about an hour later with sketches for a modified shape. From all accounts all he had done was to round off the rather angular shape and, having been accepted by John Siddeley, it was incorporated into the car.

The sands of time were rapidly running out for the Deasy name now that control of the company was, for the greater part, under John Siddeley's influence, and it had now far outgrown the early days. At the time John Siddeley joined the company there were only some 200 employees, but by the beginning of the war this had risen to 500. By the war's end the workforce had mushroomed to some 5,000, the majority being of British descent, but there were also refugees from other countries, and a large proportion of these were from Belgium. The new era which was dawning would have to cope, not only with these large numbers, but also the coming recession.

The advent of peace in Europe brought with it many problems. The efforts required to maintain wartime production orders were now replaced by the problem of finding orders to occupy the large workforce. Siddeley-Deasy was among many in this situation. All over the country, men were being laid off or made redundant, as contracts were either cut back or cancelled, and with many thousands returning to civilian life after demobilisation from the services, unemployment was rife. Of the many thousands of women employed in the armaments industry during the war, most had to return to being housewives. The relief at the return of peace brought about a boom in consumer spending, but it was shortlived, as the reality of the post-war depression became clear, much as it had been after the Napoleonic wars.

The 12 cylinder 500hp 43.5 litre water-cooled Tiger was a development of the BHP/Galloway Atlantic for production. Orders for several hundred were cancelled in 1919 at the end of the war, although two were used in the prototype Sinaia bomber.

The situation at Parkside was no better, but with Puma production continuing on a limited scale, the larger 43.5 litre 500hp 12 cylinder Vee B.H.P. engine, originally known as the Atlantic, built by Galloways, was now being produced as the Tiger. Basically it consisted of two slightly enlarged Puma cylinder banks, in cast aluminium as against the cast iron ones of the Galloway engine, on a common crankcase and with an increased bore and stroke. Orders for many hundreds had been placed, but these were immediately cancelled. Some years later it was found that some of those built were tucked away under the cowlings of innocuous looking small boats during the American prohibition era, which could show a clean pair of heels to the U.S. Coastguard if the necessity arose!

Aircraft contracts had been either completed or cancelled, and the Burlington works were being changed over to car body production for the new model. However, development work on the 14 cylinder radial was continuing, and interest was also shown by the Ministry in the two cylinder test rig for the engine. This was developed as a separate project, and finally emerged as the 3.2 litre horizontally-opposed twin-cylinder 40hp air-cooled Ounce – the smallest aero engine ever made at Parkside.

With a capacity of only 3.2 litres, the 40hp 2 cylinder Ounce was not only the first, but also the smallest aero engine designed at Parkside. It was used in a prototype Bristol Babe and also the radio controlled Aerial Target. Note the unusual valve rocker assembly.

Chapter 3
THE MERGER WITH ARMSTRONG WHITWORTH

John Siddeley had earlier decided that the company should remain in the aero engine business, and late in 1918 he had approached Daimler with a view to an amalgamation, but this fell through, and an approach was then made to the Armstrong Whitworth company based in Newcastle-upon-Tyne. They were more amenable, having been equally badly hit, and in December they agreed to negotiate an agreement with Siddeley-Deasy.

Sir W.G. Armstrong Whitworth was a very old established company dating back to 1847 when William Armstrong opened a small workshop at Elswick, near Newcastle. He was the inventor of the breech loading system for heavy guns, and combined this with the rifled gun barrel to improve the ballistic properties of shells. Joseph Whitworth is best known for the screw thread which still bears his name, and had been in business in Manchester since 1833. His own method of gun making was in competition with Armstrongs' but, following his death in 1887, the firm was bought by Armstrong, with the Armstrong Whitworth name appearing in 1897. The company began to take an interest in the building of cars in 1907, under their own name, and of aero engines in 1912, later being involved with the ill-starred ABC Dragonfly in 1917.

This engine was a triumph of salesmanship on the part of its designer, Granville Bradshaw, and was accepted with open arms by both the Government and the aircraft makers, with claims of 320hp for a weight of 600 lbs. This was a far better power/weight ratio than any competitor, but it proved to be both underpowered and overweight. The engine was also troubled with severe oscillation problems, the propeller hub being the first to suffer. Over 1,100 had been completed before the problem was recognised, other aero engines, apart from the Puma and the Rolls-Royce Eagle and Falcon, having been virtually cancelled. Despite attempts to recover the situation, the engine had been ill-conceived and was a costly failure. Armstrong Whitworth's involvement with the Puma has been mentioned earlier, but they were also concerned with the fitting of these engines into the DH.4, the mainstay of the bomber force at that time, and many of these aircraft were built at the company's Gosforth factory.

In February 1919, a proposal was made by Armstrong Whitworth to set up a subsidiary company with a nominal capital of £1,000,000 of both Preference and Ordinary shares, and with control of the company vested in their own Board. The acquisition of the Preference and Ordinary shares of Siddeley-Deasy was resolved to be for the sum of £400,000, with a rider to the effect that a top limit of £450,000 was on offer. A satisfactory agreement was effected for £419,750, to be paid in 6% non-cumulative, non-voting shares in the subsidiary company. The Siddeley-Deasy Board accepted the agreement in April, and the company was registered as the Sir W.G. Armstrong Whitworth Development Company in May 1919. Late in October the new

Puma powered DH4 built by Westlands.

company created its own subsidiary and, at a special meeting, Armstrong Siddeley Motors was formed to take over the car and aircraft business of Armstrong Whitworth and to concentrate this at Parkside. Despite the resolution adopted by his own Board in February 1919, John Siddeley was not elected to the Board of the Development Company, although he was appointed Managing Director of Armstrong Siddeley Motors.

Siddeley had foreseen the potential of commercial air travel as early as February 1917, and he asked the Board to consider the purchase of the whole of the Whitley Estate, which was agreed to if the price was acceptable, with the intention of building an aerodrome for the testing of aircraft. In this he was forestalled by the R.A.F. who had taken over the land and constructed what was in reality more of a stores depot than an airfield. It was completed early in 1918, but at the end of the war it became redundant, and in 1920 he was able to buy the site and its buildings for £5,000, although John Lloyd was not in favour, as he considered it too small and awkwardly shaped for use as an airfield. One of Siddeley's first actions was to open a flying school there.

When John Lloyd arrived from Farnborough in 1917 he brought with him the sketch plans for a modification to the RE.8 biplane. Once the design team had been set up under his leadership, the project was carried forward and eventually emerged as the Siddeley RT.1. Its first flight was in late 1917, but there was little interest and only three were built, one powered by an R.A.F. 4a, and the other two by 200hp Hispano Suiza engines. The second aircraft to be designed by the team was the SR.2 Siskin, of which three were built in sheds adjoining the London Road. It first flew in July 1919 and was one of the best of the contemporary fighter aircraft. However, like many others, it was powered by the aforementioned ABC Dragonfly and was not ordered in the recession following the war. It was to reappear in 1922 with a Jaguar engine, but was not ordered in any numbers until a few years later in a much modified form.

Aerial view of works about 1920, Gulson Road is to the right. The housing estate is in the foreground with the houses fronting London Road for foremen. Employees Institute (now St. Anne's Church) on corner of Acacia Avenue and Gorton Road (now Strathmore Avenue).

The third Parkside design was an ambitious bomber project which was eventually completed under the Armstrong Whitworth name. It was called the Sinaia and was powered by two 12 cylinder Siddeley Tiger engines. Assembly was carried out at Farnborough, but neither the aircraft nor its underdeveloped engines performed well enough, so the project was abandoned.

In February 1920, John Siddeley proposed to the Armstrong Siddeley Board that a separate subsidiary company should be set up for aircraft manufacture. The finalised proposal was put to the parent Board in April, and at the end of July, the Sir W.G. Armstrong Whitworth Aircraft Company was registered. However, initially, all design and manufacture was concentrated at Parkside, and not until 1923 was aircraft production moved to its new home at Whitley, although the design staff remained at Parkside until at least 1926. During 1923, Whitley became one of only five flying schools on contract to the Government for the training of pilots for the R.A.F. and for the reserve. It is at this point that the new aircraft company, now with its own identity and subsequent history, must go its separate way.

The Armstrong Siddeley side of the enterprise continued to expand, despite the post-war slump, with an unexpectedly high demand for the new car and, although the Puma suffered military cutbacks, such was its popularity that it continued in production for the embryo civil aviation business and for overseas customers.

Work on the R.A.F.8 engine, now known as the Jaguar, was beginning to show promise during 1919, despite interference by John Siddeley. One of the problems with the radial engine has always been to ensure adequate dissipation of the heat from the cylinders to the atmosphere. His initial suggestion was indeed very good when Heron

Third, last, and most ambitious of the Siddeley-Deasy aircraft designs was the Sinaia, powered by two Tiger engines. Only one of the two built was test flown in 1921, but problems with both the airframe and the undeveloped engines, allied to the lack of post-war Ministry interest, terminated the project. (*British Aerospace*)

was told to substitute an open-ended cylinder screwed into the cylinder head, as in the Puma, in place of the original closed-end cylinder. The cylinder head was to be fitted in a heated state so that it would shrink to a very tight fit and thus achieve a maximum metal to metal contact, which was a method destined to become almost universal within a decade. He followed this by telling Heron to substitute three horizontal valves for his cherished inclined ones. Heron thought this suggestion monstrous, packed his bags, and left for America, where he was to contribute much to the design of the Wright Whirlwind engine. He was replaced by S.M. Viale, an Italian by birth, who came to the company from Newcastle during 1919. Viale had been in the aero engine business for many years, and had been experimenting with aluminium cylinder heads and pistons in France from around 1911, but an engine of his design was unsuccessful. He came to Parkside as Chief Designer, leaving F.R. Smith virtually as Chief Draughtsman. Siddeley then proceeded to alienate Major Green by not consulting him on design changes, whereupon Green repudiated all responsibility for the engine and eventually moved to Whitley as their Chief Engineer. It was left to Viale to parry Siddeley's endless design suggestions, as Smith was easily overpowered and, in consequence, the engine went through a series of design changes until it finally emerged as a successful engine.

A supercharger designed by J.E. Ellor had been included in the original design, but it proved extremely troublesome and was redesigned by Green and Heron. Despite the improvements the idea was eventually dropped in order to concentrate on the basic engine development and, in an attempt to improve the power output, the capacity was enlarged to 24.8 litres by increasing the stroke from 5 to $5\frac{1}{2}$ inches.

To S.M. Viale must be given most of the credit for curing the original design shortcomings, and for tactfully rebuffing Siddeley's suggestions, whilst at the same time fighting for the recognition of his own.

Originally designed as the R.A.F.8, this 14 cylinder two-row engine was developed as the 24.8 litre Jaguar. Illustrated is the Mk IVC direct drive version which was rated at 400hp at 1,700rpm and used principally in the Armstrong Whitworth Atlas.

The first post-war Armstrong Siddeley car emerged in 1919 as a 30hp vehicle, with a six cylinder overhead valve engine, costing £720 for the basic chassis, the bodywork being made not only by the in-house Burlington works, but also by other coachbuilders, including British and Colonial Aeroplane Co. (Bristol Aeroplane Co. from 1920). It was immediately popular and remained in production until 1932, during which time over 2,700 were produced. At one time there were no less than fifteen types of body on offer.

Royal patronage was afforded the company in 1920, with the visit of H.R.H. the Duke of York (later King George VI) to Coventry to open the new Council House. He then came to Parkside to take delivery of a 30hp Siddeley Six and was taken on a tour of the factory by John Siddeley. Two further cars were commissioned by the Duke in 1922 and, judging from a photograph in the Employee's Quarterly for that year, there was a considerable crowd to greet his arrival at No.2 gate. Both cars were based on the 18hp chassis, which was introduced in 1921, and were a tribute to the coachmaker's art, with all timber coachwork and wood panelling. One was a rather low, pale coloured sports model with a hide leather top, whilst the other was a formal State car.

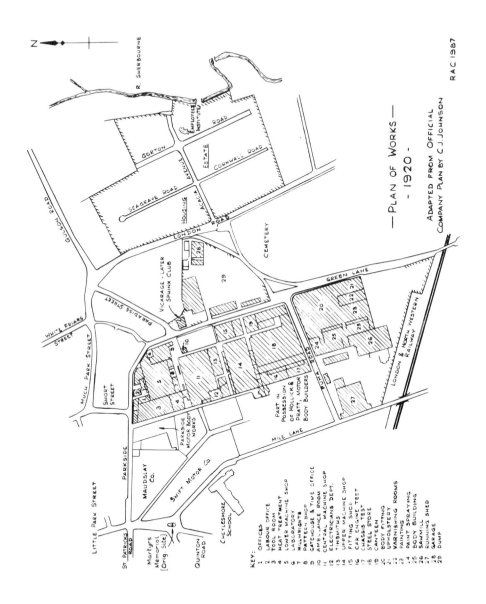

The 30hp Siddeley Six was the first post WW1 car and was introduced in 1919. This Tourer of about 1923 is a chauffeur driven one owned by Harrods. The passengers are American tourists. (*Paul Marshall*)

Whilst orders for cars increased, the cancellation of contracts for the Tiger aero engine had left a void in the workload in the design areas which the company was anxious to fill. Feelers were extended to the War Office for possible projects on the mechanisation side, and seeking interest in the potential for a projected 7 cylinder radial engine. To keep the design staff employed, one of the oddest projects ever to be undertaken by Parkside was embarked upon, which resulted in a new company being formed called Flickless Projectors Limited. However, it is almost certain that when it was registered the company had been renamed Searchlight Projectors Limited.

One of the problems with the early cinema projectors was the extremely jerky motion on the screen, caused by the uneven passage of the shutter across the film frame in the path of the light source, and its synchronisation with the film transport mechanism. An inventor by the name of G.B. Bowell had devised a system to reduce this by using a Geneva mechanism driven by an electric motor, and using a shutter in the shape of an eccentric Maltese cross. His confusing sketches and figures took some time for the Tool Design Office to sort out, since they were not skilled in what amounted to the art of watchmaking. However, after finally achieving a working mock-up, it was passed to John Lloyd and the design staff and eventually the miniaturisation problems were solved. Through keen salesmanship by John Siddeley, a production batch of 200 was put in hand. It is thought that the finished product was almost the first, if not the very first, motor-driven projector. It is known that the well established firm of Pathé were involved, and after demonstrations at the Employee's Institute in Acacia Avenue, in what is now St. Anne's Church, one was used at the old Alexandra Cinema in Ford Street, Coventry. Whether all of the initial batch was sold, or where they were made,

John Siddeley escorting H.R.H. the Duke of York (later King George VI) on a tour of the works in 1920. Photograph taken in Puma Road.

is unknown. The projector company had been set up with a nominal capital of £5,000 between the company and the patent holders early in 1920, but by October 1923 a loss of £8,500 was reported, whereupon the Board authorised the transfer of the company's holdings to John Olby of a film producing company, and nothing further was heard of it.

Despite the initial success of the 30hp car, the prosperity of the company was not improved, because, although production of chassis reached 75 per week towards the end of 1920, there were insufficient bodies to complete them. The Board records proposals for an increase in the workforce, and also the sub-contracting of body building to the Bristol Aeroplane Company who, like Parkside, had been severely hit by the cancellation of Ministry contracts. John Siddeley continued his quest for orders, and an initial one for the Jaguar was received from the Ministry in July 1920, but this was for six only, with a further six of the smaller Ounce engine. Design work had been started on a smaller version of the Jaguar, which eventually emerged as the 7 cylinder Lynx rated at 150hp; the engine being basically half of a Jaguar.

However, Siddeley was not content with the sales situation and continued to press the War Office for contracts in connection with the mechanisation of the Army. Prior to the war, he had been on very friendly terms with Lionel de Rothschild, who still had interests in the vast Vickers armaments empire, and was well aware of how important that company would become in any mechanisation, and he wanted a part in it. The earliest military work was in connection with the projected Medium D tank, for which the company had been asked to supply a modified Puma engine as its powerplant. The design of this tank had been carried out by a government department, and was a

The Duke of York (later King George VI) taking delivery of his 30hp Siddeley Six Pullman Limousine in 1920.

considerable advance on earlier designs having, for the first time, a form of independent suspension using cables which were attached to helical springs at the front and rear of the vehicle, and also a new design of latterally pivotting trackplate. A new hull shape was incorporated to give an amphibious capability. Intended for production in 1919, it was not until 1920 that a prototype was completed at the recently formed Tank Design Department under Lt. Col. Philip Johnson. Performance of the tank was good, but severe problems were encountered with cable breakage which caused the suspension to collapse, while later experiments with chains were equally unsuccessful. This type of suspension was also found to prevent it from being used in its amphibious role and, with the poor crew compartment which had evolved with the design, the concept was eventually dropped. On the engine side, the Puma gave a high power to weight ratio, but was not designed for the frequent engine speed and load variations required for cross-country use. Only five Puma powered vehicles appear to have been completed, three by Fowlers and two by Wolseley. However, it did lead John Siddeley to consider the design of specialist air-cooled engines for military vehicles.

By the end of 1920, a coal strike was affecting production and a four day week was introduced. Over half of the original production quantity of 2,000 cars had been produced, but many of these were in chassis form only, and there was considerable disquiet about the supply of bodies from both the Burlington works and from Bristol.

Orders had been received for a few three bladed welded-steel controllable-pitch aircraft propellers for experimental work, but these were not considered viable at this stage, so yet another project was dropped. These were lean times for the aero engine side of the business which was contributing only some 11% of the total sales income.

The direct drive 7 cylinder Lynx 12.4 litre engine was virtually half a Jaguar and developed 215hp at 1900rpm. Its principal use was in the Avro 504N.

However, the car body business continued to expand, the layout of the works having been improved with the long awaited opening of Puma Road as a public thoroughfare, and the modifications within Parkside itself, although the completion date for these improvements is not known.

An early 9hp Stoneleigh. The body was of aluminium on a wooden frame with a false radiator. It was familiarly termed the washtub and, on seeing it, Ernest Siddeley remarked: "Is this the b...... thing the Old Man's going to revolutionise the car world with?"

One of John Siddeley's expressed desires was to break into the light car and commercial vehicle market and, to this end, Stoneleigh Motors Limited had been formed in mid-1912, but the outbreak of war frustrated the scheme.

The advent of the first light car has already been mentioned but, following the war, the Stoneleigh company was resurrected and the Board was reconstituted under the new regime. An injection of capital was made in 1921, and a completely new model appeared early in 1922 powered by a Vee twin 1 litre air-cooled engine with inclined overhead valves and aluminium pistons. It was manufactured at Parkside, having the normal two rear seats, but with the unusual feature of the driver sitting centrally in the front. It was also made in van form with the more conventional driving position. Despite creating a good impression in the Scottish Automobile Club's Light Car Trial, where it won a gold medal, and being cheaper than the competing Rover and Austin cars, sales were poor. A slightly larger engined version was introduced in the following year, but this did not achieve popularity, while a projected 15 hp model is thought not to have been built. Production was terminated and the company died quietly in 1924, although it remained a subsidiary on paper until about 1959. Production of commercial vehicles did not re-commence after the war.

Both the Jaguar and the Ounce were on test early in 1921, and it was reported that an order for prototypes of the 12.4 litre 7 cylinder engine, now called the Lynx, had been received from the Air Ministry. Development work also began on the second new

Competing with the cheap Austin and Rover small cars, the 1.1 litre Vee-twin engined Stoneleigh failed to attract volume sales. This 1924 model has been restored and is now in the Museum of British Road Transport in Coventry.

car, a 2.3 litre 6 cylinder 18hp model. However, in March 1921, the recession finally hit the company with the completion of Ministry contracts, and a reduction in the workforce was now being planned, negotiations commencing for a further reduction in wages. These were concluded by July, but sales continued to fall.

Although the Ounce engine had been intended for the light aircraft market, one being fitted into the Bristol Babe, it was not a commercial success and was phased out in 1922. However, it did have an interesting application for the Ministry in early experiments with pilotless aircraft. These were initially designed to provide a target for aerial weapon training, an application for which Siddeley engines were to be used until well into the 1950s.

The principle of guided weapons had been experimented with for years, but it was not until 1916 that work began at the Royal Aircraft Establishment on a pilotless aircraft, using a crude spark transmitter for the remote operation of the controls. Initially it was developed for use against the high flying Zeppelins and the German heavy bombers, but it could also be used as a controlled flying bomb. Not until Sperry's gyroscope principles were adopted was a successful flight made, and this was after the war. This took place in 1921 with a converted Bristol F2B fighter, although a RAE aircraft already existed in the form of the secret Aerial Target, as it was designated. Shortly after this the aircraft was re-engined with the Ounce, plus gyroscopes and pneumatically controlled servos to operate the flying controls. Not everything went

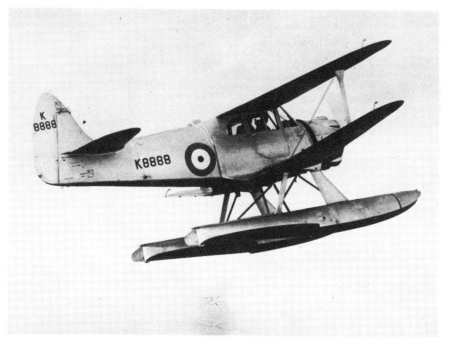

The Airspeed A.S.30 Queen Wasp radio controlled target aeroplane had a 375hp Cheetah X engine. It was also built in landplane form with a single legged spatted undercarriage. (*British Aerospace*).

according to plan, but by late 1924 most of the problems had been resolved, and it became a weapon of considerable potential. It was soon realised that a larger machine would have even greater potential, and this resulted in the Lynx powered Larynx in 1927. Development continued throughout the 1930s and culminated in the Cheetah powered Airspeed biplanes, although by this time they had reverted to their original role as target aircraft. Work on this type of aircraft has continued right up to the present day. However, in those early days, it must have been an eerie experience for anyone to find a crashed aircraft without a pilot at the controls – dead or alive! This did occasionally happen if the aircraft went out of control, or strayed beyond the range of the transmitter.

The 18hp car appeared towards the end of 1921 at a price of £575 for the chassis, and with three body styles priced at £795, £895 and £975. Initial production was to have been 20 per week, but delays in obtaining materials reduced this considerably. Mid-way through the year it was agreed to proceed with a 4 cylinder 14hp car with overhead valves like its predecessors. When it appeared in 1923, it was not considered worthy of carrying the characteristic V shaped radiator and was launched with a flat one, although still carrying the Sphinx mascot. It was to prove a considerable success, being comparatively cheap for a quality car at £360, with a top of the range price of £485.

Also in that year, one of the touring versions of the 18hp was tested by the Royal Automobile Club over a 10,000 mile run. It averaged a speed of 20mph night and day

ARMSTRONG SIDDELEY
SIX CYLINDER CARS

COMPLETE from
£595

The Armstrong Siddeley 18 h.p. Six Cylinder Saloon

"Surely a magnificent Specimen"

Prenton, August, 1924.

"DURING the past fourteen years I have owned and driven eleven cars, including British, American, Italian and Belgian. None have stood up to their work nearly as well as this 18 h.p. Saloon, on which I have now done 8,316 miles.

I am a fast driver, and have had my speedometer at over 60 m.p.h. On a tour in Scotland recently of 1,387 miles, my petrol consumption worked out at $24\frac{3}{4}$ miles per gallon, and we used one pint of oil and one pint of water.

We have had no trouble whatever with anything, and so far I have not had a single puncture.

Everything about this chassis is so practical and accessible. There is no 'fancy' work about it; but everything is there. If ever there was a 'top gear' car, this is surely a magnificent specimen, and I have on more than one occasion started up in top and gone straight up to 55 m.p.h. It is a most suitable car for an owner-driver, and can easily be looked after and driven by an elderly person."

JOSEPH BRUNDRIT, M.I.Mech.E.

Write for Booklet "F2" and address of nearest agent.
ARMSTRONG SIDDELEY MOTORS LIMITED, COVENTRY.
(Allied with Sir W. G. Armstrong Whitworth & Co., Ltd.)
London: 10 Old Bond St., W.1 Manchester: 35 King St. West
Service Depots in principal centres.

You cannot buy a better Car

OLYMPIA
Oct. 17-25
Stand 130

The second car produced by Armstrong Siddeley was the 6 cylinder 18hp of 1922. The chauffeur is Samuel Stevens who was at one time personal driver to J.D. Siddeley. (*A.S.O.C.*).

for 23 days, with only one involuntary stop for a broken ball bearing. Overall it achieved a very creditable $24\frac{1}{2}$ miles to the gallon. Whilst this was not exactly the epitome of fast travel, an earlier event in 1921 could be classed as such, when a certain Captain Dennis Shipwright won a race at Brooklands using one of the 30hp models. It was a most improbable car to attempt such a feat, but having worked hard to modify the car into a two seater by removing part of the body, the mudguards and lastly the running boards – which were integral with the chassis – he succeeded, lapping at just over 77mph. This was probably the one and only time an Armstrong Siddeley did this, and it was all good publicity for the marque.

The Jaguar engine was finally submitted to the Air Ministry 50 hour Type Test in January 1922, but a faulty crankcase caused it to be abandoned. The fault having been rectified, it successfully completed the test over a six day period in June, some nine months later than its Bristol rival. Shortly afterwards an initial order was received from the Air Ministry, and there were other enquiries from the Greek government and from America, but, in the depressed markets, sales were slow. The Ministry order was worth £18,000 and the company was anxious to begin delivery. However, labour problems arose, resulting in a dispute between the company and the A.E.U. over management functions and more proposed wage reductions. As a consequence, 750 A.E.U. members were locked out early in March, but the dispute ended after the union funds ran out towards the end of May, and the workforce returned on reduced wages.

Negotiations with the War Office had begun in March 1922 for a contract to produce a tracked vehicle known as an Artillery Dragon. Although the origin of the term is unclear, it was a variation on the normal tank concept, being designed to haul wheeled guns over any sort of terrain, and also to carry the gun's crew on bench seats in the open rear compartment, with apparently little protection. The idea was originally

The B1E1 horn steering Dragon built at Parkside in 1922/3 under the direction of H.M. Bonnaud, photographed on the London Road side of the works. Note the driver – thought to be the same as on the Pavesi photograph: page 59. (*The Tank Museum*).

conceived by a Frenchman, H.M. Bonnaud, who came to the company, with a man called Richardson, from the Department of Tank Design and Experiment at Charlton Park some months before it was closed in March 1923. Design of this amphibious vehicle was carried out at Parkside, under the guidance of Bonnaud, and featured what is known as horn steering, a device which allows the front end of the track carrying frame to pivot in a horizontal plane, a little way back from the nose of the vehicle, thus allowing the tracks to curve for steering. Three of them were to be built with the designation B1E1, powered by an Armstrong Siddeley designed 90hp V8 air-cooled engine. The initial machine was completed early in 1923 and, despite a few problems with the gearbox, it ran successfully – in a straight line ! It had, however, a distressing habit of shedding its tracks when turning and, despite many attempts, it proved impossible to cure the problem and it was abandoned, Bonnaud leaving the company through ill health in 1924. However, the project was not a total loss, since the engine had proved eminently satisfactory and was adopted for the first of the Vickers medium tanks later in 1923.

In September 1922 a large order for the Jaguar engine was received, the first since its successful Type Test, as a result of negotiations with the Greek government to power 25 Gloster Mars VI aircraft. The value of this order to Parkside was £40,000, and an additional 20 engines were ordered by the Air Ministry. The orders were regarded as a considerable coup over the rival Bristol Jupiter engine designed by Roy Fedden – later Sir Roy. This ex-Brazil Straker, ex-Cosmos Engineering engine was a 9 cylinder radial somewhat greater in capacity than the Jaguar, and also larger in diameter. After Cosmos went into receivership, Fedden considered transferring to Parkside, but Green

The Fairey Flycatcher carrier borne fighter entered Fleet Air Arm service in 1923 with a Jaguar IV engine, and had a top speed of 130mph. Three of 801 Squadron's Flycatchers are shown over H.M.S. *Furious* in 1933/4. (*MAP*)

was an implacable business rival and firmly quashed the idea, whereupon the government put pressure on the Bristol Aeroplane Company to take on the engine, and its design and development team. Having overcome Bristol's reluctance, they sat back and watched the rivalry develop. In spite of John Siddeley's efforts to drive Fedden from the map, he was unsuccessful, and towards the end of the 1920s the Jupiter was to attain pre-eminence.

Development work continued on the Jaguar to improve its power output. The Greek contract was completed by November 1922, and more orders were now coming in from the Air Ministry, who finally realised that almost all their fighter aircraft were obsolete. The first orders were for the Fairey Flycatcher, which had won a competition for a deck landing aircraft to replace the ageing Nieuport Nightjar. It went into production in 1923 with the 400hp Jaguar IV and, by 1930, when it went out of production, 102 had been produced for the Fleet Air Arm, which had become independent from the R.A.F. in April 1924. One of the Ministry requirements for the post-war air force was the introduction of all steel airframes in preference to wooden ones, and in 1922 John Lloyd had redesigned the Siddeley SR2 to this requirement, and had substituted a Jaguar engine for the original ABC Dragonfly. It first flew in 1923 from Radford Aerodrome and was now known as the Armstrong Whitworth Siskin II but, although it displayed considerable promise, it was not ordered.

Of the projects for the Army, the pioneer work by Major Wilson on tank gearboxes, by Vickers on tracked vehicles, and the success of the specialist engines being introduced by Armstrong Siddeley, now began to show dividends. The first large scale order was for the 90hp V8 to power the first modern medium tank, the Vickers Mk I, armed with a 3-pounder (47 mm) gun. The engine passed the Ministry Type Test in April 1923, giving excellent performance at low road speeds, and was eventually fitted to both the

90hp V8 air-cooled engine used in the Vickers Medium tanks, now on display at the Tank Museum at Bovington. (*Author*)

Mark I and II versions, of which some 160 were built. It was the first tank to be fitted with all-round traverse for the gun turret and some were destined to remain in service until 1940.

One extremely advanced project to use the 90hp engine was the self-propelled gun known as the 'Birch Gun' in 1924. This was basically a Vickers designed gun tractor mounting an 18 pounder gun built on to the chassis. Three experimental ones were built, and these were followed by a production batch of four, but the project was then dropped in 1930. This proved to be a very short sighted decision considering how important these 'cheap' armoured vehicles became in the 1939-45 war.

In February 1923 the company received a Ministry contract for the construction of a tracked lorry – what is now known as a half-track – based on a "Peerless or other chassis". In the event, it was an Albion lorry which was converted but, although successful, it did not lead to any production orders.

A further order was received in April for the design and manufacture of 28 Mk II Dragons. These were similar to the earlier ones, but had conventional clutch and brake steering and were again powered by the 90hp engine. In appearance they were quite neat vehicles but, as with the earlier ones, they seem to have afforded little protection for the crew. The contract was completed towards the middle of 1924 and was then taken on by Armstrong Whitworth, although the engines and gearboxes were built at Parkside.

Meanwhile, orders for the Jaguar were improving, the Air Ministry deciding to order new fighters towards the end of 1923, powered by the 325hp Jaguar III. Lloyd's persistance finally paid off with orders for the Siskin Mk III, and also the Gloucestershire

Armstrong Siddeley Small Dragon B1E2 delivered to the Mechanical Warfare Experimental Establishment in April 1924. It is shown here in modified form with Vickers machine guns. Power was provided by a 6 cyl 30hp water-cooled engine. (*The Tank Museum*).

The Vickers Medium Tank Mk II of the late 1920s powered by an Armstrong Siddeley 90hp air-cooled V8 engine. (*the Tank Museum*).

The Birch Gun 1930, the forerunner of the WW2 self propelled gun. It featured an 18 pounder field gun on a Vickers chassis with a 90hp V8 Armstrong Siddeley engine and Wilson gearbox. This is one of the second batch of four. (*The Tank Museum*).

Aircraft Company's – later Gloster – contemporary aircraft the Grebe. Both aircraft entered squadron service in 1924.

Whilst the aero engine and War Office work may appear to have taken precedence, the car work continued to progress steadily. The 14hp car continued to gain in popularity, and a production batch of 1,000 was sanctioned to add to the 500 already completed. A further batch of 500 18hp chassis was also put into production and, early in 1924, it was decided to restart production of the 30hp now that the original batch had been sold. Front wheel brakes began to be offered as an optional extra on the two larger cars, but not until early in 1925 did the 14hp receive them, following the introduction of a new chassis design which carried them as standard. Towards the middle of the year there was considerable disquiet amongst the car manufacturers when it was proposed that the McKenna Duty be repealed. This legislation was aimed at restricting imports, and its demise was expected to reduce the price of foreign cars by up to one third, giving rise to fears that it would have the opposite effect on imports. In the event, these were unjustified, allowing the price of British cars to remain almost static.

Details of the remaining Dragons built for the Ministry are extremely sparse, although available information suggests that two more small Dragons were constructed using Bonnaud's horn steering system. One of these appears to have been powered by a 60hp V4 air-cooled engine, while the other was fitted with a 30hp 6 cylinder water-cooled engine, probably the Siddeley Six car engine. Neither of them had the amphibious capability of the B1E1, and, whatever modifications were incorporated into the steering system, they were insufficient to gain further orders. Nothing more was heard of the

The B1E3 Experimental Dragon of 1925 powered by a 4 cylinder 60hp air-cooled engine. The chassis was built at Parkside but the body is thought to have been built by Armstrong Whitworth. It was disposed of to the Roadless Traction Co. of Hounslow in 1929. (*The Tank Museum*).

Designed by Henry Folland the dainty Gloucestershire Aircraft Company's (later Gloster) Grebe flew in prototype form with the Jaguar III. The production aircraft shown here had the Jaguar IV which gave them a top speed of 153mph. (*MAP*).

Car delivery in the 1920s. The car is a 4/14hp, the driver is Tony Whitehouse who remained at Parkside until 1971. Driving apparel was tailored to suit the outside temperature! (*A. Whitehouse*)

system until a variation of it, using the same curving track principle, was used for the airborne Vickers Tetrarch tank of 1937.

Having now received reasonable orders for the Jaguar, there were more to follow for the Lynx, which had been installed into the new Avro 504N, a machine designed to replace the ageing 504K as the standard R.A.F. training aircraft.

The company now began to receive further favourable publicity from the exploits of Alan – later Sir Alan – Cobham, first of all by his winning the 1924 King's Cup Air Race in a de Havilland DH.50 powered by a wartime Puma engine, although the fastest time was in fact achieved by a Jaguar powered Siskin III. Later in the year, with the same aircraft, he set up a new World Flying Record by covering the 3,000 miles to Africa and back in 54 hours. Records of one nature or another were at that time the order of the day, and a comparatively minor one was achieved in 1924, after the Oxford University Arctic Expedition transported a Lynx powered Avro 504Q to Spitzbergen, and claimed the "furthest north to date" record by flying the aircraft to beyond latitude 80° north, well inside the Arctic Circle. Basically the aircraft was a special floatplane version of the Avro 504 with a widened fuselage to incorporate a small rear cabin. After the expedition the engine was brought home whilst the airframe was abandoned, to be rediscovered in 1932 partly eaten by bears.

More overseas orders for the Jaguar materialised in May 1924 with an order for 70 engines in total for the Romanian Government, but there were to be significant changes to that engine's development before the year was out. In April the newest version passed the 50 hour Type Test rated at 360hp, but new, more stringent, tests had now been

The Avro 504N replaced the 504K in the mid 1920s as the RAF's primary trainer. Powered by a 175hp Lynx III engine it began a whole sequence of Avro trainer aircraft for the services. (*Imperial War Museum*).

introduced demanding a 100 hour test. In August one of the latest engines was submitted for this test, and over a ten day period passed with flying colours, becoming the first engine, air or water-cooled, to pass this severe trial. Its official rating was now 385hp at 1,700rpm.

In August 1924, the career began, on the shop floor, of W.F. (Bill) Saxton, father of the present Manufacturing Engineering Manager; a man destined to play a prominent role in the company's future, eventually becoming General Manager and a Director.

As far as the general work position was concerned, at the end of 1924 it was revealed that car orders were rising, the shops were also busy with the engine contracts for Tanks and Dragons, and more Jaguar orders had been promised. In December a terse statement in the minutes pointed to the next stage in aero engine development – supercharging.

One of the problems with all aero engines is that power output decreases as the aircraft climbs, due to lower air density. This had been most apparent in the 1914-18 war, when the contemporary fighter aircraft were unable to reach the altitude attained by the Zeppelins. The original Jaguar engine had gone into production with a mixing fan, which merely served to distribute the air/fuel mixture more evenly to the cylinders but, to reach greater altitudes, the mixture needed to be distributed under pressure. The first practical British supercharger was designed by J.E. Ellor at the RAE, and a version of this was incorporated in the R.A.F. 8 design. Repeated gear failures, caused by variations in the engine speed overstressing the impeller drive train, were cured by incorporating a system of centrifugal clutches to drive the impeller, which often ran at speeds in excess of 15,000rpm. Thus, in 1925, the Jaguar IVS became the world's first supercharged engine to attain production status. This form of mechanical supercharger was destined to become used by the bulk of the British, and many foreign, engine manufacturers. The alternative system to this was known as the turbocharger, whereby the impeller is driven by a turbine, driven, in turn, by the engine exhaust gas stream. This was finally left to the Americans to develop, despite the fact that both the Royal Aircraft Factory and the Bristol Aeroplane Company had earlier carried out development work on them. Whilst supercharging did not greatly affect performance at low altitudes,

(A.S.O.C.)

1930 Mk II 30hp Limousine, with Burlington body, for the wife of an Indian potentate. The car has an overall silver finish with silver and ivory fittings. All brightwork was plated with sterling silver.

it resulted in markedly improved combat ability at high altitudes, and also greatly increased the service ceiling of the aircraft.

The end of the year saw yet another epic flight by Alan Cobham in company with Sir Sefton Brancker, the Director of Civil Aviation, using the same Puma powered DH50. The purpose was to enable Brancker to attend a meeting with the Indian Government in Calcutta, Cobham making demonstration flights before flying on to Rangoon whilst the conference was in progress. The aircraft left in November and arrived back at Croydon in March 1925 after its 17,000 mile journey.

1925 saw changes to all the car models, the 14hp was given a new chassis with a lengthened wheelbase, whilst the 18hp received not only a new chassis, but also a new engine with the capacity increased to 2.9 litres. The old established 30hp continued virtually unchanged, except that a new engine was now in production with the same capacity. This featured a monobloc engine to replace the old bi-block previously used, which eased manufacture considerably.

One of the recruits to Parkside in the early 1920s was W.G. McMinnies from Temple Press. His brief was Publicity Adviser to the company, and it was not overlong before the advertising of the company became considerably less conservative, and in some instances even humorous. In pursuit of his aims he was to make the cars climb almost impossible mountains and, just to prove the origin of the product, three demonstration cars, one red, one white and one blue were used. Shortly afterwards he was to coin the slogan "cars of aircraft quality", which could hardly be justified on the grounds of performance, though the quality of the cars was unquestionably good. Nevertheless, it was new and adventurous advertising.

More publicity for the company accrued in 1925 when Siskin aircraft were first and second in the King's Cup Air Race, and Alan Cobham, having hardly set foot in the country, was planning his next venture. This was the long flight to Capetown to survey a suitable route for the planned Imperial Airways service to South Africa. For this journey, the company provided a Jaguar engine for his DH.50 and also a gift of £1,000. Several cars were also supplied to cover the ground side of the survey. Leaving Croydon

Alan Cobham on the River Thames in 1926 at the completion of his 26,000 mile out-and-home flight to Australia in his Jaguar powered DH50.

in October, the survey took four months, Cobham returning in March 1926 to a hero's welcome for the 17,000 mile flight and with praise for the company's products. Also in 1925, the 7 cylinder Lynx radial engine attained production status, following a contract being obtained by A.V. Roe for the new R.A.F. training aircraft, the 504N.

Almost immediately, Alan Cobham prepared to set off once again on one of the most spectacular flights of the decade, in attempting the 28,000 mile round trip to Australia. His intention was to leave early in May, but a strike at Parkside, in support of the miners, curtailed the overhaul of the engine and it was not until 30 June that he finally took off from the River Medway in his well tried Jaguar powered DH.50, fitted for this journey with floats. He achieved this long and hazardous flight in just over 61 days, despite being unaccustomed to floatplanes, the return journey taking only 24 days. He alighted on the Thames close to the Houses of Parliament on the afternoon of 2 October. Only three days later it was announced that King George V had been pleased to confer a knighthood on him. There was, however, tragedy attached to the flight, when his famous mechanic, A.B. Elliot, was hit by a Bedouin bullet over Arab territory and died shortly after reaching hospital in Basra. There is no question that Cobham would have wished Elliot to be with him on that eventful October day.

The influx of orders for the Jaguar, and an increase in the output of the 14hp car to 150 chassis per week, had stretched the capacity of the workforce to the point where, in the two months from November 1925, it had risen by 700 to almost 3,600. Not only was it envisaged that production of the 14hp should be reorganised to rise to 200 per week, but there was now development work on the next aero engines to be considered. These emerged later in the year as the 60hp 4.1 litre 5 cylinder Genet, and the 125hp 8.9 litre 5 cylinder Mongoose.

Design work had begun at Vickers in 1922 on a new heavy tank known as the A1E1 Independent, and in 1925, Parkside was asked to design and manufacture the 350bhp 35.8 litre V12 air-cooled engine to power it. The tank was delivered to the War Office in October 1926, and featured a main turret mounting a 3-pounder (50 m/m) gun and

To comply with the rules of the 1926 Daily Mail trials at Lympne, the standard DH 60 was fitted with the 75hp Genet and became the Genet Moth. This example appears to be one of six supplied to the R.A.F. Central Flying School for their aerobatic team. (*British Aerospace*).

four wing turrets housing 0.5 machine guns. Although it had an excellent performance for its day, it was adjudged too expensive by the impoverished War Office and only one was built. However, this was not the case in the tank conscious Russian Army, where the design of the tank itself was copied as the T35 and ordered in fair numbers, although it was outmoded by the outbreak of the 1939 war. The original tank now resides in the Royal Armoured Corps Tank Museum at Bovington.

On demonstration at Camberley in 1926 for the Dominion Premiers Conference, the A1E1 heavy tank used a 375hp air-cooled V12 engine, but only one was built and this is now in the Tank Museum at Bovington. The small tracked vehicle on the left is a one-man Carden-Loyd carrier. (*the Tank Museum*).

Solid tyred Pavesi tractor for the War Office on test on Whitley Common in 1929, probably for demonstration purposes.

In May 1926, talks began for the transfer of the licence to build Pavesi tractors from Armstrong Whitworths to Parkside. Armstrong Whitworth had obtained the licence in 1925 from the Italian, Ing. Ugo Pavesi, who had designed this rather odd vehicle around 1914 for agricultural use. Basically it was a heavy tractor with four wheel drive and larger than usual wheels, in most instances with solid tyres, and was steered by being able to pivot in the centre of its two part chassis through a multi-directional universal joint, no form of road springing being provided. A small number were produced for the military in 1925 by SA La Motomeccanica, after which production was taken over by Fiat at Turin, where considerable numbers were produced from 1926 and used by the Italian Army well into the Second World War. Armstrong Whitworth appear to have done little with the licence, and it was acquired by Parkside in the first half of 1927. The first imported example appears to have disliked being delivered to an alien country, and quite literally dropped in. As the Siddeley representatives watched, it fell from the crane and disappeared into the murky depths of Liverpool docks, to be eventually salvaged suffering from severe seawater corrosion.

Late versions of the 4.1 litre Genet 5 cylinder engine, designed in 1927, developed 80hp and weighed 203 lbs. Captain Bremer's Junkers A50 used this engine for his overland flight round the world.

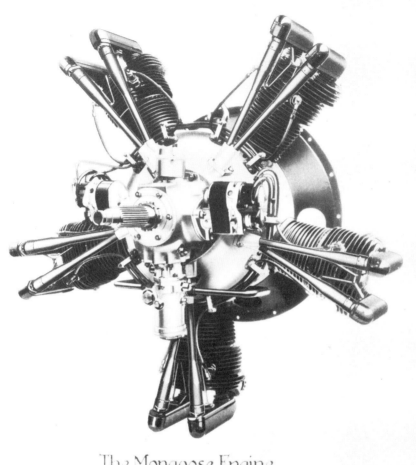

The Mongoose Engine.

Introduced in 1928 the 8.9 litre 135hp Mongoose was virtually a 5 cylinder version of the Lynx aimed at the light aircraft market, but although technically successful it was not widely used.

Chapter 4
THE ARMSTRONG SIDDELEY DEVELOPMENT COMPANY

Towards the end of 1926 events were moving very swiftly towards yet another Company restructuring. Strangely perhaps, as mentioned earlier, John Siddeley had not been elected to, nor even nominated for, the Armstrong Whitworth Development Company Board in 1919, and was thus unable to exert any influence on that company. Armstrong Whitworth had been badly hit following the war due to their almost total reliance on Ministry work, and in 1925/6 John Siddeley became concerned at the profits of the Coventry based companies being used to support an ailing parent. He was finally elected to the Board in 1926 and was now able to appreciate the full implications of the situation. Not only were the Coventry profits being used as support, there were those of yet another subsidiary, the electrical firm of Crompton and Co., also being used. This situation was intolerable to Siddeley, and he finally decided to act when the parent company lost millions of pounds on an abortive paper mill project in Newfoundland. He immediately contacted the local branch of the Midland Bank and put his proposals to the manager. His personal friendship with the chairman of the bank, Reginald McKenna, enabled him to leave with the promise of a large unsecured loan, without

The Armstrong Whitworth Argosy Mk I City of Glasgow, one of three to enter Imperial Airways service in 1926/7. The Argosy Mk II of 1929 was fitted with the more powerful geared Jaguar IVA engine in cowlings. (*R.A.F. Museum*).

Powered by a Jaguar III the 1924 Armstrong Whitworth Siskin Mk III had a top speed of 134mph and a service ceiling of 20,500 ft. Experiments in 1925 to increase performance resulted in the fitting of the experimental cowling shown. Despite an increase in speed of some 4mph, cooling problems were encountered and it was soon removed. (*J.W.H. Hiscocks*).

formal agreement. He promptly offered to buy the Development Company in November 1926 for £1,500,000. One of the conditions stipulated was that the parent company was not to undertake the building of either aircraft or cars. Although the parent Board were averse to this, the prospect of a large cash injection was more than tempting, and in December a deal was concluded.

John Siddeley was now firmly in control of the Development Company, although he remained on the main Armstrong Whitworth Board until, in March 1927, he relinquished his position as Managing Director, and finally resigned his ordinary directorship in 1928.

In March 1927 he called an Extraordinary General Meeting of the Armstrong Whitworth Development Company for the purpose of changing the company's name to the Armstrong Siddeley Development Company, and it was disclosed that apart from holding assets in both Armstrong Siddeley Motors and Armstrong Whitworth Aircraft, the new company also held 250,000 shares in the aforementioned Crompton and Company at Chelmsford. Armstrong Whitworth, for their part, were not long to survive as a separate company and became part of the Vickers Group in 1928. It is perhaps ironic that if Siddeley's gamble had failed he might well have found himself back with Vickers, whom he had left some 20 years previously.

The new Board was constituted in February 1927 when John Siddeley was elected Chairman of the company, and on 14 March the company's seal was affixed to the document whereby they retained the use of the name "Armstrong" in the company's title. One of their first tasks was to consider a suggestion by the Agents for Lord Cheylesmore that the company should purchase the freehold of the site, but it was not

Salmons coachwork adorns this neat little 1926 4 cylinder 14hp Mk II Drop Head Coupé, familiarly known as the Doctor's Coupé. (*Author*).

proceeded with. One significant personnel movement prior to the split with Armstrong Whitworth was the arrival in 1926, from the Newcastle works, of H.T. (Tom) Chapman to join the engine design section. He was also destined to play an important part in the company's later affairs.

Orders for the Jaguar continued, output now being concentrated on the supercharged version for the newly redesigned Siskin IIIA. John Lloyd had reworked the all steel-framed fuselage and, although the ground level performance showed little improvement, when the aircraft entered squadron service in May 1927, with the 450hp supercharged Jaguar IVS, its service ceiling had been raised from 21,000 feet to 27,000 feet.

By the middle of 1927 there was a reduction in demand for cars, but work was continuing on engines for the medium tanks, and it was proposed that once the existing orders from Vickers had been completed, the company should endeavour to obtain further contracts by direct negotiations with the War Office. It is reputed that some time in 1927 a vehicle with rear wheel steering was developed for the War Office. What purpose it would have served is unknown, but, whatever was intended, it would have been extremely difficult to drive. In the event, no record of its having been received by the Army Experimental Establishment has been found.

Whilst the old 30hp and 14hp cars remained in production, there was a considerable change in the mid-range vehicles. For the 1927 Motor Show the old 18hp 2.9 litre car was now advertised as a 20hp, available in both long and short chassis versions with four body styles, while a new 15hp 1.9 litre 6 cylinder car was introduced. Top of the range prices were £425 for the 15hp, and £385 and £500 respectively for the short and long chassis coach built saloons. The new car was in the traditional perpendicular style, with a high, well furnished body, and the multi-studded disc wheels which were a

Now owned by a member of the A.S.O.C., this immaculate 1928 Mk II 4/14hp carries a Burlington Lonsdale Saloon body. (*Author*)

feature of all the Siddeley cars until well into the 1930s. However, the company now introduced a side valve engine for this model, although an overhead valve engine was retained in the 20hp. Although a seemingly retrograde step, it was very much in keeping with other manufacturers. In line with most of the motor trade, slight reductions in price were introduced for all models, although all had now been improved by the addition of a central chassis lubrication system, and automatic advance-retard for the ignition.

The early months of 1928 were fraught with problems for the car industry as orders began to fall dramatically, and there was talk of amalgamations in order to reduce the effects of both the recession, and the import of foreign cars. Many advertisements from this period onwards carried the Union flag and the 'Buy British' slogan.

Although work on the Pavesi tractor had begun with the final transfer of the licence, the military side of the business continued to be spasmodic. The first of the tractors was delivered to the Experimental Establishment in May and was obviously successful, with the result that a batch of 20 was put into production late in the year. Engines were still being made for the Vickers Medium tank and for the Dragon version, and the company received a further contract from Vickers for the development of a 180bhp V8 air-cooled engine for use in the experimental A6E2 and E3 tanks, the "16 tonner", with an armament of one 3-pounder gun and 5 Vickers .303 machine guns. Only three of these were built – the third having a Ricardo engine – the first Siddeley engined one being delivered in May 1928. The engine was also used in the three experimental Vickers designed Medium Mk III tanks in 1930, which were derived from the A6 series, one being built by Vickers, and the other two by the Royal Ordnance Factory.

For the 1928 Motor Show a new 12hp 1.2 litre 6 cylinder car was shown. Like its predecessors, it had side valves and, despite its depressing performance, it was well to

1929.

The Armstrong Siddeley 15 h.p. 6 cyl Fabric Saloon, price £360.

ARMSTRONG SIDDELEY
SIXES
THE NEW 15 H.P.

THE ideal car for the Owner-Driver—especially the lady—the Armstrong Siddeley 15 h.p. Six is the best medium powered, full-sized family car on the road at a modest price.

Easy to drive, economical to run, simple to maintain. Handsome coachwork of first quality, fashioned on modern lines, attractive two-tone colour schemes.

Engine of Aircraft quality. Lively performance. Light steering. Perfect brakes.

You cannot buy better value. A trial run will convince you. Arrange one to-day. Cars on view at all our Agents.

Fabric Saloon, 6 lights   £360 complete
Coachbuilt Saloon, 6 lights   £395 complete

Write for Catalogue A54
ARMSTRONG SIDDELEY MOTORS LTD. COVENTRY
LONDON : 10 OLD BOND STREET, W.1
MANCHESTER : 35 KING STREET WEST
Agents in all principal towns

BUY BRITISH AND KEEP YOUR COUNTRYMEN EMPLOYED

Note the "*Buy British*" slogan – this exhortation was to be found on most advertisements in the later 1920s and well into the 1930s. (*A.S.O.C.*)

Converted Armstrong Siddeley 20hp car for advertising the Wilson pre-selector self change gearbox 1932. Coventry Garage at rear used to stand on the bottom corner of Holyhead Road in Coventry.

the forefront of the fashionable trend for small 6 cylinder cars and sold well. Like the 14hp car, which was phased out in 1929, it was not considered worthy of the familiar Vee radiator, but it was nevertheless a quality car, selling in its cheapest two seater form for around £250.

The most significant technical advance on the company stand was the self-changing pre-selector gearbox. For the origin of this important innovation we must return to 1901, when W.G. Wilson was associated with the Wilson-Pilcher car, which used a clutchless transmission and an epicyclic gearbox. Wilson-Pilcher was bought out in 1904 by Armstrong Whitworth, whereupon Vickers, who also had an interest in Armstrong Whitworth, took note of its military potential. Wilson enlisted in the Royal Naval Air Service in 1914, and was closely concerned with the design and production of the first tanks, attaining the rank of Major before the conflict ended. After the war he received the C.M.G., and was awarded £7,500 by the Royal Commission on Awards to Inventors in recognition of his work, which he used to carry on with the development of the transmission system for the motor car, as a replacement for the crash gearboxes normally fitted. Work continued on the military side, but by 1922 he had built a smaller version for cars. He then had to persuade one of the motor manufacturers to fit and try the new gearbox, a task which he found extremely difficult.

Having waited so many years, he suddenly decided to patent the gearbox and sold the rights to a third party. However, Vauxhall Motors decided to fit one to a demonstration car late in 1922 but, with motoring history within their grasp, they were taken over by the American General Motors company in December 1925 and the new gearbox was pushed to one side. This was too much for Wilson, who took court action to regain total control of his patent and, very much against the odds, won his case. John Siddeley had long been looking for something of this nature to add further refinement to his cars. He had briefly flirted with a Lanchester epicyclic system earlier in the 1920s but, having purchased one, found it far too complicated for economic production. Hearing of Wilson's court action, he arranged a meeting in 1927, the outcome of which was the formation of Improved Gears Limited in December 1928 with a nominal capital of £10,000, and with Wilson and John Siddeley as joint Governing Directors. The main aim of the company was to grant licences under Major Wilson's patents.

At the Olympia show that year the 20hp car was offered with a three speed Wilson box as an optional extra at £35, or with a four speed one at £50. Although it made the cars heavier than before, it proved to be a boon, especially to the lady drivers of the day, and to those not well skilled in the art of double de-clutching. It proved a tremendous advance to the technology of the day, whilst the attendant audible whine of the epicyclic gears, as they were braked by the selector brake bands, and a certain harshness in the actual change, were a comparatively small price to pay. It was left to Daimler to add the final refinement when they married it to their new fluid flywheel under licence. Many of the boxes were fitted to racing cars in the 1930s, and also to commercial vehicles and some marine projects. In 1934 the company changed its name to Self Changing Gear Trading Company, and eventually became part of the Longbridge empire.

By 1928 the Jaguar was beginning to show its age, and although now supercharged, and available in geared form, it had been overtaken in the race for higher power by the rival Bristol Jupiter. The gearing of engines was not a new concept, and had been adopted as a means of achieving increased power by using higher engine revolutions, and then gearing the propeller shaft down to maintain optimum airscrew speed. With

Designed as a replacement for the DH50J in Australia, the DH61 Giant Moth was offered with a variety of engine options. Shown here is the Jaguar powered version. The last of this hard worked type was written off in 1935. (*British Aerospace*).

The prototype Armstrong Whitworth Atlas Army Co-operation aircraft powered by the 400hp Jaguar IVC.

the exception of the Genet and Mongoose, all the Siddeley engines were ultimately to be available in this form, also being supplied supercharged if required.

The Jaguar was, however, still in demand because of John Siddeley's insistence that all Armstrong Whitworth aircraft were to be powered by Parkside engines. In consequence, it was fitted in the production Armstrong Whitworth Atlas two seat biplane, which was the first aircraft to be designed from the outset for Army co-operation, and whose production run was to outstrip the Siskin. In order to keep up with the greatly increased power now being demanded for military aircraft, the 48.6 litre 750hp 14 cylinder Leopard was designed, much on the lines of the Jaguar, and passed its flying trials successfully in late 1928. The production engine was rated as one of the most powerful in the world but, despite this, it failed to achieve large scale production. In 1929 it was joined by its smaller brother, the 27 litre Jaguar Major (renamed Panther in 1932), and the 13.6 litre Lynx Major, both of which were basically the parent engine with an increase in the cylinder bore from 5" to $5\frac{1}{4}$", and were rated at 525hp and 260hp respectively. The Lynx Major was to be far better known as the Cheetah, the name which was adopted from 1930 onwards.

By this time, John Siddeley's rigid attitude in dictating engineering policy was beginning to become something of a liability now that engine design and development was becoming more scientific. With the total eclipse of the Jaguar imminent, the Bristol company were pushing development of the Jupiter to its limits. They were also experimenting with the sleeve-valve as a means of simplifying both engine manufacture and build, and also the increased cylinder efficiency which would accrue by eliminating the problems associated with conventional valves, and valve spring failures.

The captive A.W.A. market may have been a source of self satisfaction, but it became noticeable that the bulk of aircraft built by them for the smaller military aircraft market were for prototypes only, or for very small quantities, and there was no serious attack on the civil market. As a result, neither the Leopard, Panther nor the Tiger, which appeared in 1932, were built in large quantities. The problem with this situation, which was to be almost immediately compounded, was that engine development work was severely retarded. How much of this can be directly attributed to John Siddeley's

The 48.6 litre Leopard. When introduced in 1930 it was one of the most powerful engines in the world at 700hp but was not noted for its reliability. This was the only Siddeley engine to feature 4 valves per head, although the final version reverted to two. Note the open valve gear.

attitude is impossible to say, but one can be sure that the Parkside designers wept bitter tears as the Bristol company forged ahead in the design race for the higher powered, prestige, radial engines. Nevertheless, the company accountants were happy with large orders for the smaller engines, and it was this market on which Armstrong Siddeley became dependent. That the Jaguar had been an excellent, reliable, engine is beyond question, and its half brother the Lynx inherited all its good qualities, as did the newer Cheetah engine.

The compounding referred to earlier occurred in May 1928, when the Development Company acquired A.V. Roe and Company from Crossley Motors. The aircraft side of this business had been declining for some time, and they had expressed interest in a merger to John Siddeley, whilst Crossley's were known to be unlikely to oppose this suggestion. Siddeley was more than interested in the proposition, because it would

One of the original Ju.52 aircraft was fitted with an 800hp Leopard engine, and is shown here in its seaplane form. This aircraft is better known in its famous tri-motor form during the 2nd World War.

ensure production of the Lynx continuing into the foreseeable future for the Avro 504N, and any subsequent primary training aircraft. As a result of the discussions, an agreement was reached and Siddeley purchased the company for something in the region of £250,000, with the transaction becoming a very profitable one for the Development Company.

A second company to join the fold in 1928 was the old established firm of Peter Hooker Limited, which had been responsible for engine sub-contract manufacture on a considerable scale during the war. In recent years they had been supplying pistons to Armstrong Siddeley and, after the firm ran into difficulties, they approached John Siddeley for a loan of £10,000. This sum was soon absorbed, and twice more Wallace Devereux, of Hookers, approached Siddeley for further loans. The result of this was that a company called High Duty Alloys was set up with Devereux as Chairman, thus again proving the business acumen of John Siddeley, having acquired for a mere £30,000 what was to prove another highly profitable company.

Whilst these new companies were being absorbed into the Development Company, there were also changes within Armstrong Siddeley itself. 1928 saw the appointment of John Siddeley's eldest sons, Cyril and Ernest, to the Board. Cyril Davenport Siddeley was born in August 1894 and appears to have joined the company after the Great War, in which he served in the Royal Warwickshire Regiment until 1918, being twice mentioned in despatches. After joining the company he seems always to have been most closely concerned with administration and sales. He eventually became Sales Director, but remained very close to the car side of the business up to the 1939 war, during which he again served with the same regiment until 1945, attaining the rank of Colonel. He rejoined the company and finally resigned on the grounds of ill health at the end of 1952.

Ernest Hall Siddeley was born in October 1895 and joined the company in 1913. He enlisted in October 1914 and rose to the rank of Lieutenant in the Royal West Kent

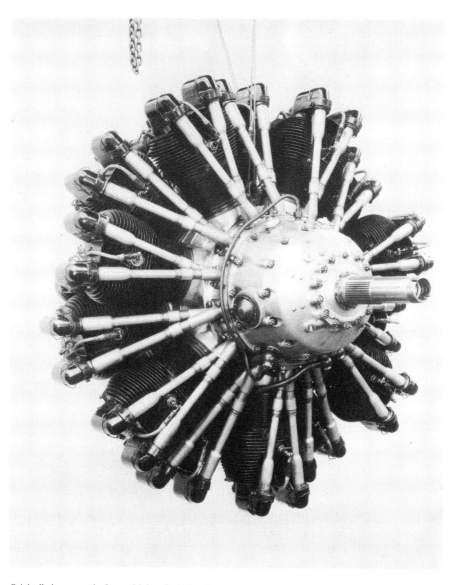

Originally known as the Jaguar Major, the 27 litre Panther, introduced in 1930, was designed to produce 500hp. Shown here is the geared Mk IX of 625hp. The most used version was the IIA in the Fairey Seal for the Fleet Air Arm and the R.A.F.'s Fairey Gordon.

Regiment, seeing service in the Loos salient and the 1916 Somme offensive, until being invalided out towards the end of 1916 with that most prevalent First World War complaint – Trench Fever. After a spell in America in 1920 to study the latest trends

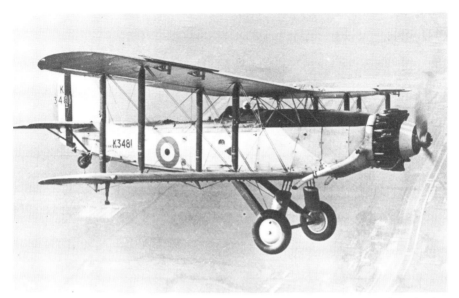

Fitted with the 525hp Panther IIA engine the Fairey Seal bomber-spotter-reconnaissance aircraft for the Fleet Air Arm began life as a converted Fairey III F. It was also produced as a float plane, and, in both forms, also served with the R.A.F. as the Gordon. (*MAP*).

Designed by Roy Chadwick in 1929, in anticipation of a replacement R.A.F. primary trainer, the Avro 621 was the forerunner of the successful Avro Tutor. Originally civil registered this aircraft entered R.A.F. service as shown, with the cowled 155hp Mongoose IIIA. (*British Aerospace*).

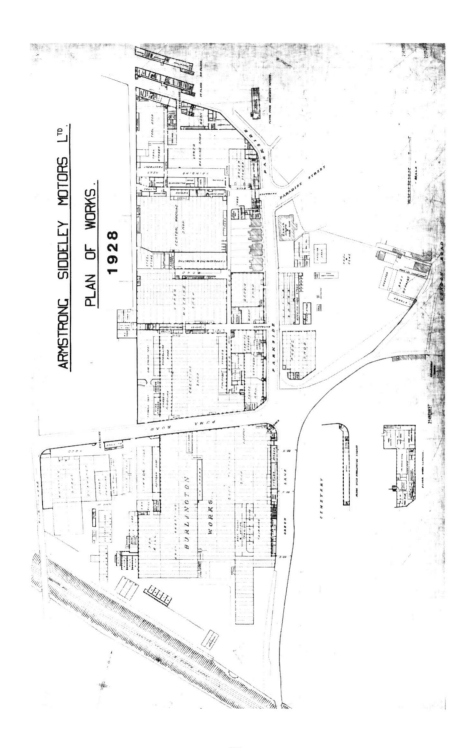

One of the many oddities in the late '20s and early '30s was this propeller driven Hydroglider powered by a 7 cylinder Genet Major. There is nothing to indicate its origin but it would certainly have been unpopular with the neighbours.

in car manufacture, he returned to become assistant to A.G. Asbury and, in 1922, he became Superintendent of car testing and finishing. He appears to have enjoyed experiments, and one of these was to find out what happened if a downshift of the Wilson gearbox was attempted at speed. He soon found out – the rear axle broke! One of the more successful ones was with hydraulic tappets, which were fitted to several models in the 1930s. Becoming Technical Director (Cars) in 1932, he remained with the company into the Hawker regime after his father left in 1935, but was not very happy and finally left the company in June 1937. He returned only once to Parkside, and then only after a personal invitation from H.T. Chapman, the then Managing Director, after the war.

There were other senior personnel changes too. A.G. Asbury died in May 1928 and was succeeded as Works Manager by F. Baron, but he was not destined to remain overlong, and departed for Bristol following an argument with John Siddeley. Not for the first time, as output began to drop, did wiser counsels prevail and he was persuaded to return, and remained until his death in 1931.

In May 1929, negotiations were well under way to acquire a new sports ground in what is now Siddeley Avenue. The earlier sports facilities were situated on the south side of Crabmill Lane, off the Stoney Stanton Road, on land originally owned by the Coventry Ordnance Works. These were very cramped, and it was appreciated that a move to a more spacious site would be advantageous. The 30 acre site was conveyed to the company by T.D. Griffith in July for £5,510, and a loan of £5,000 was made available from the Athletic Organisation for the building of a pavilion and for laying out the grounds. In December 1929, John Siddeley had reached agreement with the Bishop of Coventry for the conversion of the Employee's Institute in Acacia Avenue to become St. Annes Church. He had acquired the property privately in 1923 with this eventual goal in mind, but now he had to request the Board to release him from the

Eight wheel, twin bogie, Pavesi tractor for the War Office powered by a 60hp five cylinder Genet aero engine. 1929. (*The Tank Museum*)

clause whereby it would revert back to the company, so that it could be taken over by the Ecclesiastical Authorities.

The efforts by the company to expand its range of aero engines continued, the 5 cylinder 5.2 litre 100hp Genet Major appearing in 1929, with an increased bore and a $\frac{1}{2}''$ increase in the stroke over the earlier Genet. Along with several others the company were also investigating the compression ignition (diesel) aero engine, and intensive development of a slightly larger engine than the Leopard was carried out. This engine appears to have been under development for airships, but work ceased following the R.101 disaster at Beauvais in 1930, as also did all work on rigid airships.

The first Pavesi tractor for the War Office was delivered in May 1928, and was a four axle version built by Fiat in Italy with a Pavesi gearbox and, in all probability, a Fiat engine. Whether this was a replacement for the Liverpool docks survivor is not known. This was one of the heavy tractors with a pair of twin axle bogies in place of the standard two axles, each axle being fitted with four pneumatic-tyred wheels. Interest by the War Office was rather lukewarm, although there appeared sufficient promise for them to order the standard version and a second multi-wheel vehicle powered by a Genet engine. This latter was given the designation B10E1, and was delivered to the Mechanical Warfare Experimental Establishment in November 1929 at a cost of £3,500. There were no follow-up orders, however, although the vehicle remained on strength until it was sold to J. Lyons of Chester in 1934, but its ultimate fate is unknown. Five of the standard version were delivered, commencing in October 1929, with solid tyres, at a cost of £1,500 each, whilst a standard vehicle was supplied to India at £2,250. The only other delivery was a standard pneumatic-tyred reconnaissance car in February 1930. The engines for these were a 45hp 4 cylinder air-cooled engine designed at Parkside.

It is known that at least 11 of the batch of 20, put into production earlier, were completed, but with little interest being shown by the British Army, prospects of overseas sales were extremely slim. It is thought that no more were made and the licence

Flexibility of the Pavesi is amply demonstrated in this 1929 shot of the eight wheel Genet powered version.

was not renewed at the end of 1931 or early 1932. One of the three unsold machines – probably a standard one – is reputed to have been sold to a building contractor at Bromley, as being the only vehicle capable of site haulage. The fate of the remaining two is unknown, but it is likely that at least one of these was supplied to Italy to demonstrate the Wilson gearbox, although any potential sales were blocked by Italian interests.

Although designed for heavy haulage over uneven ground, it was just not equal to the demands made of it over the terrain the War Ministry had in mind. Its comparatively high centre of gravity did not help matters, and it is known that the first one imported rolled over, killing the officer driving it.

Having secured a seat on the Board, Ernest Siddeley was appointed Technical Manager (Cars) in late 1929, whilst F.R. Smith became Technical Manager of aero engines and special projects. The Jaguar Major was now in the throes of Air Ministry testing, and there was another overseas boost when an order for 30 Genets came from Germany for the Junkers Junior aircraft, which provided excellent publicity for the company some time later. F.R. Smith was not to hold the post of Technical Manager for long, and it was a sad loss to the company when he died in the first half of 1930 at the early age of 48. His design work, on both the Puma and the Jaguar, had taken the company from its infancy to a position of high esteem in the aero industry throughout the world. Together with F. Baron, who had been responsible for all engine test work until his death in September 1931, he had been closely involved with the development and ultimate success of the Jaguar. Smith's position as Chief Draughtsman was taken by A. Magson.

The production of tank engines continued, but now the company was asked by the Ministry to develop two more air-cooled designs for new projects. The first of these was a 120bhp V8 engine for a medium tank designated A7 by the War Office. Two were produced for the A7E1 and E2, but the third prototype, E3, was fitted with twin AEC diesels. The first of the three was delivered to the Experimental Establishment in

Pneumatic tyred Pavesi reconnaissance vehicle of 1930, powered by an Armstrong Siddeley 45hp 4 cylinder water-cooled engine, photographed on Parkside.

November 1932. The tank had been designed by the Ministry and built at the Royal Ordnance Factory at Woolwich, and was among contenders for a replacement for the erstwhile Vickers Medium, which was still in production. However, with the continuing impoverished state of the War Office, no production orders were forthcoming. They were retained for development purposes and many design features were incorporated in the Matilda Infantry Tank Mk II of 1939, although power for this was supplied by commercial diesel engines.

The second engine was a 25hp air-cooled twin-cylinder built for use in the Carden-Loyd Mk VI and VIA Tankettes, designated B11E. These were essentially a means of carrying a machine gun over ground being raked by small arms fire, a task they performed extremely well. It was built, or modified, for various roles, but only three are known to have been powered by Armstrong Siddeley engines.

A third engine was commissioned by Vickers for their private enterprise Six-Ton light tank, which was designed in two versions; the 'A' version having two machine gun turrets side by side, and the 'B' with a single turret mounting a 47 m/m (3 pounder) gun. The engine, developed at Parkside, was an air-cooled horizontally mounted one of 87bhp with 4 in-line cylinders. The tank appeared in 1930 and, though totally ignored by the British Army, was used by other countries, Poland being probably the biggest customer with a total of around 50. Other countries bought a few, including Russia, who promptly tested it against their own designs and, finding it superior, immediately put it into production – both tank and engine – as the T26, of which some 12,000 were built. One can only imagine the anguish of the Vickers and Armstrong Siddeley

Horizontally mounted 87bhp air-cooled engine for the Vickers 6 ton tank and Dragon. This is a late production version for overseas c1938, possibly for delivery to Finland. Cylinder construction was based on that of the aero engines.

accountants as the copies rolled out of the Russian factories. These three were the last of the Parkside designed specialist engines for Army mechanisation, but another potentially lucrative business was at hand now that John Siddeley and Major Wilson had joined forces. This began to be realised when the third Vickers Medium Mk III was fitted with the Wilson gearbox in October 1929, along with the Parkside built Pavesi's.

Before leaving the 1920s, the company completed a contract for several 30hp omnibus chassis for use by Imperial Airways towards the end of the decade, despite having been out of the commercial vehicle market for many years.

The Wilson gearbox had proved extremely successful in the 20hp model, and it was now extended to the 15hp side valve engined car from May 1930. For the Olympia Show later in the year, it was decided that all the models in the range should have them as standard, with the exception of the 12hp, which would still have the option of a manual change box. A variety of body options still remained, the 12hp being offered with a choice of four styles, whilst the 15hp and 20hp had five. The old 30hp was now nearing the end of its long run (being phased out in 1932) and was offering only a limousine body, or a more expensive version of the same configuration from Hoopers at £1,575. Several specialist body makers, including both Hoopers and Mulliners, were now supplying the company in addition to the Burlington ones, more especially for the higher priced models. Some bodies for the smaller cars were supplied by Hoyal, whilst

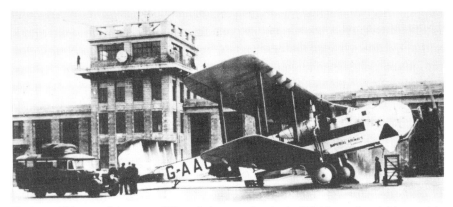

The Jaguar IVA powered Armstrong Whitworth Argosy at Croydon in 1932. The coach on left is one of the extra long Siddeley 30hp chassis supplied to Imperial Airways. Another of these vehicles was used by Lufthansa. (*from a postcard by Pamlin Prints*).

some featured Weymann type fabric bodies. With the exception of the manual 12hp, all the range were now fitted with Triplex safety glass, although it was an option on that model. Both the 12hp models were offered with wire wheels as an alternative to the standard disc ones, and all models had the option of front and rear bumpers at £5; strange perhaps, but Ernest Siddeley had a rooted aversion to bumpers as a standard fitting, regarding them as the hallmark of a bad driver.

The original 1236cc engine in the 12hp had such a dreary performance that one was despatched for testing to Ricardo's at Shoreham. For the many-paged report they charged £600 but, at the end, apologised, saying there was little they could suggest to improve it. However, in 1931 it was replaced by a 1.4 litre engine and the car regained a measure of respectability. At the same time it was considered that the de-luxe models were worthy of the familiar Vee radiator, even though it was merely a facade to hide the flat core. In this revised form it proved very popular, the two seater version selling for £285, whilst a neat piece of advertising by McMinnies was to catalogue the Coupé version as especially suitable for "Daughters of Gentlemen".

In 1930, Daimler were granted a licence for the Wilson gearbox, and by combining it with their fluid flywheel created the classic Wilson transmission line. Armstrong Siddeley took on a reciprocal licence for the flywheel, but its virtues were only apparent on the larger engines. Daimler promptly proceeded to patent the combination without informing John Siddeley, and began to put all manner of difficulties into supplying the fluid flywheels to Parkside, and, after some twelve months, supplies ceased altogether. The incident had its effect on Siddeley, and also affected his relations with Wilson for a considerable time. However, despite some doubts as to the validity of the patent, and the apparent monopoly it afforded to Daimler, it was never challenged.

Generally speaking, the range of Armstrong Siddeley cars, with the odd exception noted previously, had little regard for performance, but were second to none for reliability. This was convincingly demonstrated in the 1931 Monte Carlo Rally, when the specially equipped 20hp Silver Sphinx carried off the Grand Prix d'Honneur as the best equipped and most comfortable car in the rally. Whilst it could only win the rally if the cars starting from Stavanger, in Norway, or from Athens, failed to finish, it

The Best Advertisement for ARMSTRONG SIDDELEY CARS
is the cars themselves

WE know that we make the best six-cylinder cars that are made, but that mere statement—truthful as it is—in no way is comparable with a ride in one of our Cars. Words cannot convey to you the ease of driving or the comfort in riding that a trial run can give you. We have official agents in every town. Go to yours and go for a ride. Let the Car tell you the story. The Agent will be glad to give you the test and leave it to you—because he knows he sells, at its price, the best.

Ask him, particularly, to demonstrate our proved self-changing gear.

J. D. Siddeley
Chairman
Armstrong Siddeley
Motors Ltd. Coventry
London: 10, Old Bond St., W.1.
Manchester: 35, King St. West.
Agents in all principal towns.

Write for Catalogue P.I.

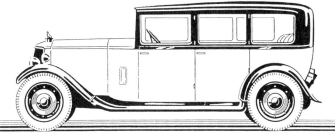

The Armstrong Siddeley Special 20-h.p. Enclosed Limousine or Landaulette, with self-changing silent four-speed gear—£885. *As illustrated.*

This fine 6-7 seater provides road travel of the most luxurious kind. It is highly attractive in appearance and very spacious in the accommodation provided.

You cannot buy a better Car

A Mulliner bodied short chassis 20hp Coupé of about 1930.

Although the smaller models did not carry the familiar Vee radiator until post 1931, this 1930 2 seat Drop Head Coupé was still a very neat vehicle. The radiator shell now has the painted finish introduced for the 1930 Motor Show.

A 1931 model 12hp Caludit Coupé for an eastern Prince.

For 1931 the 12hp range was fitted with a new 1.4 litre engine to replace the earlier 1.2 litre, and a new bonnet line. Shown here is the Coachbuilt Saloon.

*A touch with the finger—
A press with the foot.*

Gear changing is now a pleasure –

with the

ARMSTRONG SIDDELEY

SELF-CHANGING, SILENT FOUR-SPEED GEAR

This *proved* self-changing four-speed gear is fitted to

All motorists—both experts and novices—have longed for a perfect, noiseless gear. That is exactly what Armstrong Siddeley has produced. This silent, self-changing four-speed gear, apart from making motoring much more pleasant, ensures a higher average speed. It makes driving safer and much more economical. It allows more room for occupants of the front seat.

But in order to realise fully the wonderful advance this four-speed gear has made in motoring, it is necessary to see it actually in action. Any Armstrong Siddeley agent will be glad to show it to you. See it to-day.

ARMSTRONG SIDDELEY CARS

ARMSTRONG SIDDELEY MOTORS, LTD., COVENTRY
London: 10, Old Bond St., W.1.   Manchester: 35, King St. West.
Agents in all principal towns.   *Write for Catalogue P.3.*

(A.S.O.C.)

nevertheless maintained the required 25 mph average for the 3,500 mile route and was first to the control at Monte Carlo. Its highest rally honour was to finish 3rd in the hill climb section against much bigger and more powerful cars, whilst it finished 4th of the cars which started from John O'Groats.

Despite being technically successful, the Mongoose aero engine did not enjoy a great measure of commercial success, and appears to have been discontinued in 1935/6. By using the converse of the Jaguar/Lynx concept the 17.7 litre Double Mongoose appeared in 1931, a 10 cylinder two row radial rated at 340hp. It was this engine, designed under the wing of H.T. Chapman, which featured in the shadowy "Mongoose Affair". During early engine runs it suffered from severe high frequency vibration problems at the front end of the crankshaft. John Siddeley was not used to suffering this undignified phenomenon and said so, at which point it seems that Chapman was prepared to resign, but was persuaded to stay on. Eventually the problem was referred to an outside consulting engineer, and a multi-fingered spider, sprung into pockets in the front casing, and whose hub provided a small extra crankshaft bearing, finally cured the trouble. In its modified form the Double Mongoose was renamed Serval and was used in the Armstrong Whitworth Atalanta airliner for Imperial Airways. However, like its predecessor, it did not enjoy a great deal of success. Also in 1931, a 7 cylinder Genet Major, based on the 5 cylinder engine, appeared.

The outcome of the Mongoose Affair was the transfer of Chapman from design to production, and a position under the new Works Manager, C.S. Oliver, who had joined the company from Humber where he had held the same position.

Prior to this, the death of F. Baron had resulted in a man called Hutchinson becoming Works Manager, but he offended the religious principles of John Siddeley with an announcement that the factory would be open on Good Friday. This was anathema to the deeply religious Siddeley, with the result that Hutchinson was soon replaced by Oliver. Indeed, the traditional Good Friday holiday has only recently been abandoned. John Siddeley, however, was absent for a large part of 1931, being injured in a serious motoring accident towards the end of the year. He was away for several months, and only returned in January 1932 after convalescing on the South Coast, although he came back to the works for a short spell towards the end of the year, despite not having fully recovered.

Armstrong Siddeley remained in the forefront of the smaller aero engine market by virtue of the excellent publicity afforded by the exploits of the solo pilots of the day. In 1931, a Finnish pilot, Captain Bremer, piloting a German Junkers Junior powered by an 80hp Genet, had won the first prize in a race around Sweden and, in 1932, he won a similar race around Europe, later piloting the aircraft from Helsingfors to Capetown and back. With the same aircraft, in 1934, he attempted to fly overland around the world, travelling by ship across the Pacific and Atlantic oceans. Leaving Helsingfors on 16 May he arrived in Tokyo on 9 June, travelling on to America in a Japanese steamship. On 20 June he arrived in New York after crossing the American continent, and embarked for Bremerhaven. Arriving there on 28 July, he flew on to London and Paris via Malmo in Sweden.In the course of this epic flight, he traversed 22 countries and, what is even more remarkable, taking into account the size of both aircraft and engine, is the fact that he had no blind flying equipment nor special features, and, after Istanbul, no air speed indicator either. Despite being covered in dust whilst flying over a large proportion of Asia, and negotiating storms, fog, rain and mountains, Captain Bremer was lavish in his praise of the Genet which had given no trouble throughout.

The 1931 20hp Silver Sphinx in Monte Carlo at the end of the arduous Monte Carlo Rally. The crew, left to right, are 'Sammy' Davis, Whitlock and Stafford.

The Lancashire singer Gracie Fields in America in the early 1930s. The car is a 20hp Rally Tourer.

Chassis erecting shop in April 1930. The build line on left appears to be for the 12hp model. This area is now part of the RB.211 No.2 Shop.

The aero engine build – now RB.211 No.2 Shop – in about 1930. The engines appear to be late production Jaguars.

The Serval IV, a ten cylinder two row engine of 17.7 litres. This geared engine developed 340hp at 2,000rpm and was used in the Armstrong Whitworth Atalanta of 1931.

A small problem arose for the company in July 1931, after it was reported to the Board that Bristol had been using Siddeley patents on supercharging for some time without permission, presumably in connection with the use of centrifugal clutches. A letter was read, drafted by the company's Patents Agent, which was to be sent to Bristol and the results reported at the next meeting. No further reference to this appears in subsequent minutes, and it must be assumed that an amicable settlement had been reached.

The country was almost at the height of the depression in 1932, and throughout the year many workers were laid off. Parkside was only one of many plants affected. Car production had always been rated as modest at Parkside, being of the order of about 3,000 per year, and a batch of 700 similar cars was considered mass production. Somewhat surprisingly, the year proved to be one of the best ones for sales! A new 20hp car was announced early in the year to replace the earlier model, and with it the company began to revert to overhead valve engines, whilst there was an increase in

Imperial Airways Armstrong Whitworth Atalanta, powered by four Serval engines. The aircraft illustrated is the first of the class and went into Imperial Airways service late in 1932 with a speed of 130mph and a range of 400 miles. (R.A.F. Museum).

capacity from 2.9 to 3.2 litres. Road testing was carried out thoroughly, as usual, and Cyril Siddeley decided that the car should be used for rally work, as was its predecessor. Three works cars were entered in the 1932 Alpine Trial, initial snags having been overcome, with a fourth entered privately. Of the three works cars, not one lost a mark over the 7,500 mile event, whilst the privately entered one lost only two. Although not winning the event, the awarding of three Glacier Cups to each works entry was considered a very satisfactory outcome. One of the original three cars – registered KV 2000 – is still extant. Further prizes were gained in the R.A.C. Rally of that year, where the works cars, of several models, gained three awards for excellence of coachwork, eleven special plaques, two of the principal rally prizes and a further award for the best performance in the over 1100 cc class.

Probably the most significant event of the motoring year occurred at the Olympia Show, where a surprise exhibit was the new Siddeley Special, which could certainly justify the 'cars of aircraft quality' slogan. With the old 30hp model now gone, its replacement was of the same capacity, 4960 cc, but the engine was constructed largely of Hiduminium, a high grade aluminium alloy much used on the aero side for crankcases, pistons and cylinder heads. The company's experience with this material was of great value in the design and manufacture of the engine, although its ancestry was apparent by retaining the same bore and stroke as the older engine. The car was fitted with a four speed Wilson pre-selector gearbox as standard, because early tests with a crash change box were abandoned after they had shown clutch pedal operating pressures to be impossibly high. There was none of the sluggish performance of the old 30 either, with its ability to cruise quite happily all day at 65 mph, whilst the short chassis version could comfortably reach 90 – 95 mph. Despite being an easy car to drive, it was incapable of fast gear changes and needed preselecting well in advance. Nonetheless, it was a superb and much under-rated car priced at £950 upwards, and was to prove a top contender on the rally circuit.

It was even considered for the 1933 Le Mans 24 hours race, but in this highly competitive event, for which a Siddeley had never been entered, it was feared that failure would undermine the company's image.

In the mid 1930s, the 7 cylinder 150hp direct drive Genet Major MkIII acquired a new design of cylinder head, with cast-in rocker boxes, and with steeply inclined valves to aid cylinder scavenging. Casting problems, however, restricted its use to only this engine, the geared Mk IV and the short stroke Cheetah XI.

The Genet powered Junkers A50 Junior was used by Capt. Bremer on his overland round the world flight in 1931. This photograph well illustrates the corrugated skin construction used by the Junkers concern.

The long chassis 20hp Sports Tourer of 1932 with the prototype Jaguar Major (later renamed Panther) powered Armstrong Whitworth Atlas Mk II. Surprisingly, despite official records, the aircraft still carries its original registration letters.

By 1932 the 12hp car had received the traditional radiator shape carrying the revised Sphinx emblem. The Drop Head Coupé shown has Maltby coachwork.

Development work on the aero-engine supercharger had continued over the years, and in 1932 Armstrong Siddeley became the first company to introduce the two speed supercharger. This was a device whereby the pilot could select the higher gear ratio as altitude increased, thus extending the range of altitude over which the engine power could be maintained. A new engine, the 32.7 litre Tiger, appeared at the end of the year and was another 14 cylinder two row radial rated at 725hp, roughly midway between the Panther and the Leopard. However, it was still basically a boosted Jaguar and, due to the current workload on the smaller engines, development was not pushed very hard and it failed to realise its potential; indeed there is a school of thought that none of the three higher powered engines were a technical success, being based too much on the Jaguar. One of the problems with the two row radial was that of vibration, due to the long unsupported length of the one-piece, two-throw forged crankshaft between the main bearings, and the larger the engine became, the greater the problem. The solution was to use a split crankshaft and a centre bearing, but this was not adopted within the industry until the mid 1930s.

It may be that the quest for reliability was the major factor that resulted in none of the three being pushed to their limits in development, whereas the single row engine was, e.g. the Bristol Jupiter and the later Mercury. Whatever refinements and improvements were incorporated, there was no substitute for vigorous development in the quest for higher power, and it is likely that this led to the design of the later three row engines as a means of overcoming the inherent limitations of the stretched Jaguars of that time.

Whatever the facts, the Tiger was to achieve a comparatively fair production quantity, and in its Mk VIII form, geared and supercharged, it reached a rating of 860hp in low

Cabriolet coachwork by Salmons, of Newport Pagnell, is carried by this 1932 15hp with a 6 cylinder side valve engine.

Still carrying the upright Sphinx mascot, this is the 20hp Sports Saloon for 1932 fitted with a sunshine roof.

At £1,250 the most expensive in the range was this beautiful 1933 Siddeley Special Limousine.

Sir Malcolm Campbell's 4.9 litre Siddeley Special Sports Tourer with Burlington body.

The Hon. Cyril Siddeley's 1934 Siddeley Special with Vanden Plas coachwork. Note car in foreground !

gear at 6,250 ft, and 780hp in high gear at 14,250 ft. It was fitted in the Blackburn Shark and Ripon for the Fleet Air Arm, in which it gained a good reputation for reliability, and the early marks of the Armstrong Whitworth Whitley, until it was superseded by the Rolls-Royce Merlin. It found a civil application in the Armstrong Whitworth Ensign of 1937, but was undoubtedly underpowered for this, the largest British airliner of the day.

The most significant personal event of 1932 occurred in June with the publication of the King's Birthday Honours list, in which a Knighthood was conferred on John Siddeley for his services to the mechanical development of the armed forces. There was also more expansion of the plant, almost three acres of land and workshops being acquired from the Swift company. This portion of land was later known as the old Swift dump, and extended through to Mile Lane from the Parkside end of the present computer block and, in the other direction, from Puma Road down to the present boundary with the Climax company. The lease cost the company £4,250.

Licensing by Improved Gears continued, and amongst the companies to obtain them were Clement-Talbot, Sunbeam, ENV Engineering, AEC and the Drewry Car Company, whilst Major Antonio Lago (of Lago-Talbot fame) was persuaded to take on the Continental and American rights for the idea. All of which contributed royalties for Armstrong Siddeley, who were already producing them for Riley's at the rate of 100 per week. For Major Wilson it was the end of a long battle as the market rapidly expanded, and shortly afterwards he became Managing Director of ENV. Perhaps the highest accolade was either its adoption by the famous ERA competition concern, or

With a capacity of 32.7 litre, the Tiger VIII was the first production engine with a 2 speed supercharger. It was rated at 845hp at 6250 ft. in low gear and 760hp at 12,750 ft. in high gear. With a maximum of 920hp for take-off it weighed 1290 lbs and powered early marks of the Armstrong Whitworth Whitley.

for the fleet of omnibuses for London Transport. Parkside was also finding an external market for its car engines when the 20hp engine was adopted for the last of the Burney Streamline cars in 1932/3.

Work began in 1932 on one of several experimental aero engines to be built at Parkside. This was called the Hyena, with 15 cylinders in five in-line banks of three, and was the first of the 3 row engines. The valves were operated by five between-bank camshafts, driven by gears from the crankshaft, from which short pushrods operated the valve rockers. Its over-square cylinders had a total capacity of 26.6 litres and it was designed to have a rated output of 620hp at 2250rpm. It should be noted that engine nomenclature had now changed from cat names – although to be zoologically accurate, the Genet, Mongoose and the later Civet are not of the cat genus, but are nevertheless cat-like and also carnivorous – to those of the dog family, and eventually seven names were to be used or proposed. The reason for this is unclear, but it is known that an engine called the Mastiff, a large 14 cylinder two row radial designed for Italy, and the much later Deerhound, were both metric engines and it is thought that all the dog names, including the Hyena, were also metricated. It is unfortunate that nothing further is known of the Mastiff, but what went on in the experimental area next to the old tool room, now part of Product Centre C9, was forbidden territory, even to the Works Manager.

First of the second batch of Blackburn Shark Mk II torpedo-spotter-reconnaissance aircraft for the Fleet Air Arm, powered by the 760hp Tiger VI. Whilst the majority were landplanes, the aircraft shown was one of several carried on the D II H catapults of the battleship *Warspite* and the battlecruiser *Repulse* prior to the war. Many of the type remained in second line service into WW2. (*Imperial War Museum*).

The Hyena was flight tested in the AW. XVI, replacing a Panther engine, and appears never to have achieved its designed output. There were also problems in cooling the rear row of cylinders, despite several alternative layouts being tried. Accounts recalled by the Armstrong Whitworth test pilot, Charles Turner-Hughes, indicate that, although the engine was rather heavy and prone to overheating, its basic design was nevertheless sound. It is thought that only one, or possibly two, were built, but the overheating problem seemed insoluble and its development ceased. Of the Mastiff, it is known that at least one was built, photographs of it being extant, but whether it went beyond the test stage, or what its power rating was, is at present unknown. It is known, however, that when the latter engine reached the Jig and Tool D.O. all dimensions were promptly converted to Imperial measure for the design of the tooling – possibly the first occasion, but certainly not the last !

The possibility of acquiring the freehold of the Parkside site had been considered by the Board in 1926, having been approached by the agents of Lord Cheylesmore and, at that time, it was agreed to leave the matter in abeyance. In March 1934, John Siddeley reported to the Board that the question had arisen again, and that he had been given the opportunity to purchase the whole $30\frac{1}{4}$ acre site, including the area under lease to other companies, bounded by the railway, Mile Lane and Parkside, together with the stretch of land already in their possession between Parkside and the London Road. The asking figure was £35,000, which the Board agreed to and a cheque was made out for a 10% retainer. The purchase was completed by early December and the Land Registry Form filed.

The frontage of Armstrong Siddeley from Short Street. This 1930s photograph shows little change from that of the original Iden Company taken some 25 years earlier. *(from a postcard courtesy Les Neil)*

With the recession still biting, the prices of the cars remained reasonably steady but, in order to attract more overseas business, it was agreed to drop the price of the 12hp chassis from £140 to £125. For the more sporting coupé versions of the car there was still the option of wire wheels instead of discs. This version weighed just over a ton, but offered a quiet 60 mph for a comparatively modest £285. The bodywork had now begun to change, the exposed luggage grids on the saloons being concealed within the swept tails. In August the second of the new overhead valve models appeared. This was the 17hp, a 2.4 litre 6 cylinder with a choice of three wheelbase lengths, In its lightest form it weighed 28½ cwt, and body options were available to suit all kinds of customer, from a rather well proportioned sports coupé to a compact limousine selling at £585. A new feature was the fitting of permanent hydraulic jacks, known as the Jackall System, into the 15hp. These had originally been fitted into the Silver Sphinx for the 1931 Monte Carlo rally. A further refinement was the fitting of leather rocker box covers to reduce noise.

The rally year was to be the one of the spectrum: the works team for the 1934 R.A.C. Rally consisted of nine 12hp sports cars each painted a different colour. Cyril Siddeley was team chief and it was arranged that, all being well, a rendezvous of 8 o'clock in the morning would be suitable but, much to everyone's surprise, the rainbow began to form just after dawn, Miss Roper's violet one being the last to arrive. It was said in the publicity that if she had failed to arrive, the only excuse which could be offered was that the car was painted infra-red, and was thus invisible. However, all was well, and

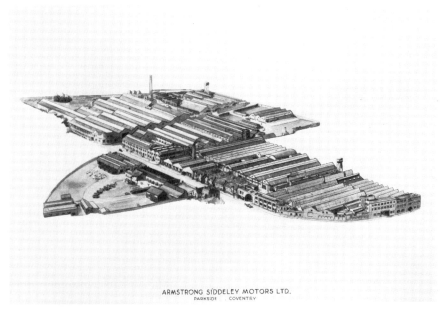

ARMSTRONG SIDDELEY MOTORS LTD.
PARKSIDE , COVENTRY

View of Parkside c1935. Original Iden works on extreme right. Note Puma Road still in use as a thoroughfare, and cottages between 2 and 3 gates still in private occupation.

no cars lost marks in the final examination. Cyril Siddeley was awarded second prize in his class, whilst in the coachwork class, a private entry, a 20hp Silver Sphinx II, won first prize in the £500 to £700 4 door saloon class.

There was criticism of the company early in 1934, when questions were asked in the House of Commons, over a contract which had been negotiated with the Nazi government in Germany for the supply of a number of Panther engines. Despite this, the Minute Books record nothing untoward, and it appears that the contract was completed.

The 7 cylinder Genet Major reappeared in a new guise towards the end of 1934 after it was modified for the Ministry and became the Civet. In this form it was used in the Cierva C30, one of the later Cierva autogyros. The autogyro was the subject of a 1920s patent by Juan de la Cierva y Cordorniu, a Spaniard, for a rotating wing aircraft not unlike a helicopter in general form, but totally different in function. The rotor was, in effect, a horizontal windmill, normally rotated by the action of the air and, in its early form, it required forward motion to turn the rotor until a speed was reached to generate sufficient lift for take-off. In the C30 the concept had been taken a stage further, in that the engine could be coupled to the rotor to attain take-off speed and then disengaged. A short forward motion and the machine was airborne, landing being accomplished purely by windmill action, whilst control in the air was effected by tilting the rotor. It had a small tailplane and narrow fins above and below the fuselage, purely for stability. Some 70 of the C30A version were built and became familiar sights in use for police traffic observation at major sporting events.

Amongst the body options on the larger cars was the Limousine, photographed here at Charlecote Park on the long 20hp chassis.

This 12hp Sports Tourer of 1934 carried a price tag of £268. It was first introduced for the R.A.C. Rally in March of that year.

The Avro Rota autogyro, designated C30A, was powered by a 140hp 7 cylinder Genet Major. With a top speed of 100mph and a cruising speed of 75mph, it had a range of 250 miles. The rotor, shown folded here, had a diameter of 37 feet. (*MAP*)

The 1935 12hp in Tourer form. This photograph was taken at the 1987 A.S.O.C. National Day at Shendish House. (*Author*)

A more modern version of the Sports Saloon is this 1935 17hp. It featured a very narrow centre pillar to the side windows. (*Paul Marshall*).

Typical of the mid 1930s Saloon body styles is this 20hp of 1935, now owned by a member of the A.S.O.C. (*Paul Marshall*).

The beginning of 1935 saw the advent of yet another new and varied project for the Parkside workforce. In the early 1930s, the French Michelin Tyre Company had developed a pneumatic-tyred railcar for operation on many of the smaller railway branch lines, and some fifty were in operation by 1935. As a measure of their success, one car in the Lille area was regularly covering 360 miles per day and maintaining a continuous daily service. In the course of this work, one had amassed an impressive 130,000 miles, whilst two others were over the 100,000 mark.

They were typically French creations from a major national company, and in theory had two basic advantages, superior adhesion and a smoother, quieter ride. One of the French Type 11 railcars – in appearance more akin to an articulated motor bus – was tried out in the Oxford area in 1932, and some interest was shown by both the Great Western Railway and the London Midland and Scottish Railway. A second car of a new design ran trials in 1934 on the L.M.S. and, as a result of these, John Siddeley set up the Coventry Pneumatic Railcar Company in association with Armstrong Siddeley Motors and plans were made for two of the cars to be made at Parkside.

A special shop was set up adjacent to Parkside, later to become the Admiralty torpedo-engine shop, under the managership of L.W.R. Robertson and construction began early in 1935. Evidence suggests that the car was designed at Parkside based on the French Type 20 railcar, but tailored to suit British conditions. The mainly aluminium 13 litre, water-cooled, overhead valve V12 petrol engine was designed and built in the works and developed 275bhp, power being transmitted to the one driven bogie through a Wilson gearbox. The car was designed, like the French one, to carry 56 passengers and around a ton of luggage. In order to keep the bodywork as light as possible it was made up of pre-formed flanged aluminium panels made in Nuneaton by the Midland Sheet Metal Company. The flanged edges were bolted together with a strip of rubber between them to ensure a measure of flexibility on uneven track, and to reduce vibration.

A feature of the eight wheel bogies was the fitting of a sensor to each tyre so that, in the event of a loss of pressure, a warning would sound in the driver's cab. Jacks were built in, and it was reputed that a wheel change could be achieved in only a few minutes. Special shoes were fitted carrying high frequency current for operating the track signalling circuits without direct rail contact.

The first of the red and cream bodied vehicles finally emerged – or almost did – on 20 June 1936. The hitch occurred when it was found that the 55ft. car was too long for the existing width of Parkside. First the London Road side boardings went, and then part of the cycle sheds, before it was finally swung out into the road – all this under the anxious gaze of the Coventry Gas Company team, whose lamp standards were in grave danger of demolition. It was towed by tractor on two road bogies to Coventry goods yard where it was transferred on to its railway bogies. Its tare weight was a mere $10\frac{1}{2}$ tons in running order, and this, combined with the pneumatic tyres, gave it remarkable acceleration and braking, whilst a comfortable 70mph was easily attainable. Its light weight, due to the necessity of keeping the load on each tyre to a minimum, was to cause problems when the L.M.S. asked the company to fit normal railway couplings and buffers. This would have increased the weight considerably, but fortunately it was not pursued.

Following initial trials on the old London and North Western Railway branch from Rugby to Market Harborough, a press run was made from Rugby to Wansford on 28 July. Both cars were put into public service on 14 September on services centred on Coventry to Rugby, Nuneaton and Leamington, and from Rugby to Leamington direct.

Technically it can be said that the two cars were a success, but the attitude of the railway companies was only lukewarm and they were not purchased by the L.M.S.,

The Coventry Railcar nearing completion in 1936, with its workforce. The manager, Mr. Richardson, is seated centre in the dark suit. (*R.A. Clarke*).

Daylight at last for the first Coventry Railcar on 20 June 1936 fitted with road bogies. The problems began a few minutes later. Surprisingly the towing tractor is still shown as one of the Norman Box fleet, although the company had been taken over by Pickfords in 1929. (*copy of Peter Whitehead print*).

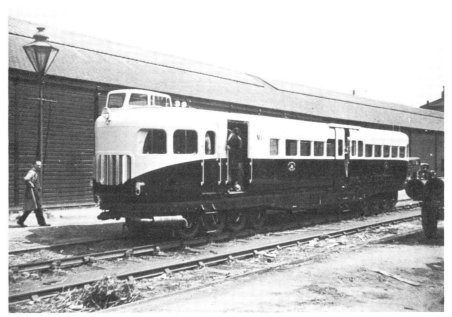

After shipping its rail bogies the Coventry Railcar posed for photographs and carried out some short demonstration runs in Coventry goods yard opposite Spencer Park. (*copy of Peter Whitehead print*).

Coventry Pneumatic Railcar No.1 approaching Kenilworth from Coventry in 1936. Note the beautiful ex-LNWR repeater signal behind the car. (*Gordon Coltas*).

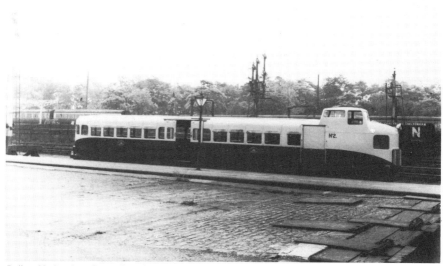

Railcar No.2 at Leamington Spa (Avenue) LMS Station in 1937. The shutters at the front of the car were for radiator cooling air. (*Gordon Coltas*).

Railcar No.2 leaves Kenilworth for Coventry in 1937. The raised roof shutter by the side of the driver's cab was to provide radiator cooling air when running in reverse. (*Gordon Coltas*).

The Burlington car assembly shop in 1935. The area is now the RB.211/Development Shop.

nor were any further orders received. The ride has been described as superb, but the quietness and the gentle rolling motion could induce a form of travel sickness. They were thoroughly disliked by the track maintenance gangs who referred to them as the 'silent death', whilst there was a complaint from an irate local farmer that the new fangled toy and its hunting horn were upsetting his hunters. One of the technical problems was that of tyre wear caused by the multiplicity of points and rail joints that the car had to negotiate on these local lines, whereas in France they were used on longer branch lines with fewer rail breaks; indeed they are still in use on the Paris Metro. Unfortunately no comparison figures are available for the two countries.

Economically, however, there were two principal drawbacks. One was that for a company like Armstrong Siddeley, with no previous railway experience, they were too large to be manufactured at an economic price, and, even at this period, there were viable alternatives in service. The G.W.R. had put a railcar into service in February 1934 built by Hardy Rail Motors (A.E.C.), with Park Royal bodywork, powered by a commercial diesel engine. This was more solidly constructed and could carry the same number of passengers on half the horsepower of the Michelin, although their later cars used twin diesels of almost comparable power to the Michelins, but were more versatile. Even with twin diesels, they were not only cheaper to run, but were more substantial and cheaper to construct. However, it must be said that the whole concept of railcars was never really accepted in this country until the revenue from the branch lines began to decline in the 1950s, and the railways moved into the Beeching era. The cars continued to run in revenue earning service until late in 1937, but were then moved into storage at the Michelin factory at Stoke-on-Trent, where they were broken up in 1945.

This was the final project to be undertaken during John Siddeley's chairmanship, and another restructuring was already in motion.

Chapter 5
THE FORMATION OF HAWKER SIDDELEY AIRCRAFT

By 1935 John Siddeley was approaching 70, and his unbending attitude to engineering policy began to prove a handicap to the company now that more precise standards were available for both design and development. This had manifested itself most strongly in the continued endeavour to stretch the basic Jaguar design to a point beyond its capability, along with emphasis on the development and production of the smaller engines. There seems little doubt that, as with the cars, the ultimate quest was for reliability and, in this respect, the Parkside products were as good as any other. This left the design team with an insoluble dilemma, and the result of this apparent neglect was that the development of the high power radials now rested firmly, at least in this country, in the hands of the Bristol camp, although the Tiger had some success in the medium power range.

The captive Armstrong Whitworth and Avro market seemed satisfactory enough, but even here his policy had its opponents as they strove to keep pace with the competition. In November 1933 there was a heated argument between Siddeley and John Lloyd, after Lloyd had suggested another company's engine should be fitted to the Armstrong Whitworth Scimitar instead of a Parkside product. His obvious preference led to him being summarily dismissed but, once again, wiser counsels prevailed and he was reinstated in the following January.

John Siddeley also had an avowed wish to maintain a personal contact with the workforce. In the early days, a canteen get-together had been easy – whether it was to praise or berate – but, as the company had grown to some 2,500 employees, it had become for several years past, almost impossible.

Much to the surprise of many of the senior management of the various companies, to the industry generally, and to most, if not all, at Parkside, John Siddeley sold his interests to Hawker Aircraft. It was a move he had obviously been contemplating for some time, although it only became known following the disclosure that discussions with Handley Page had fallen through. Details of the sale have never been revealed, but it appears that the central figure in the negotiations was a financier called Philip Hill, who had been attempting to arrange a merger between Hawkers, who had recently taken over the Gloster Company, and the Bristol Aeroplane Company. After Bristol opted out of the deal, Hill, having heard of the failure of the Handley Page negotiations, approached John Siddeley.

A deal was concluded in July 1935 between Siddeley and T.O.M. (Tom) Sopwith (later Sir Thomas) of Hawkers, whereby a new company – Hawker Siddeley Aircraft – was to be set up to acquire the whole share capital of 419,751 ordinary £1 shares in the Armstrong Siddeley Development Company. John Siddeley was not on the new Board, but he agreed to his name being retained in the new company's title and

A 1934 photograph of Sir John Siddeley with the still extant 1904 Siddeley car.

remained Chairman of the Development Company until he formally resigned on 30 September 1936. In 1937 he became Lord Kenilworth, and purchased Kenilworth Castle for the nation in the same year. He left the town for good not long afterwards, but remained in contact with the industry until his death in Jersey in 1953. His son, the Hon. Cyril Siddeley, remained in residence in the castle gatehouse until 1958 and, on his departure, presented the freehold of the entire castle to the Urban District Council. It is now in the care of the Department of the Environment.

In retrospect, what can be said of John Siddeley's influence on the fortunes of Parkside? He was an autocratic man and a strict disciplinarian, and had the fiery temperament which is often found in those of shorter stature. He was also able enough to overpower any opposition by the force of his personality. Despite this, he was generally regarded as a fair, generous and often kind man as circumstances warranted. His confidence in his own ability was considerable, and there is little doubt that he would have few qualms in outflanking his competitors and, in his early days, his superiors. One of the problems in his years at Wolseley was that the Board found that the Wolseley name was all too often subordinate to that of its General Manager – John Siddeley – and this could not be tolerated.

It was his business acumen which was his most powerful weapon. One example of this can be found after the First World War, when the establishment decided that the new rich amongst the industrialists, who had contributed so much to the war effort, had become both too rich and too powerful. The Excess Profits Tax which was levied on these industries involved enormous sums of money but, whilst some companies foundered under the pressure, he had the ability not only to weather the crisis, but to increase the prosperity of the company.

John Siddeley was in business for profit, for both himself and his company, and this he achieved by astute dealings and a knack of predicting market trends. He was also prepared to work hard for success, and demanded the same of his employees. If the works became slack, he was not averse to taking on new and totally different contracts and projects and expected the workforce to adapt to them. He was a very private man, who rarely granted interviews, and there is very little known, and ever likely to be known, of his private life. He was, however, a great benefactor of the Coventry Hospital, and to other aspects of city life, although this was known to few at the time.

Thus did the Siddeley era come to an end, the simple fact being that the company had outgrown the man. However, the Parkside story continues with C.S. Oliver being appointed General Manager.

Another contract which was now showing considerable promise had been undertaken as long ago as 1928, after the company was invited by the Admiralty to take an interest in the production of torpedo engines, gyroscopes and other work for the new Mk VIII 21 inch submarine torpedo which appeared in 1927. These comparatively small 4.59 litre 4 cylinder radial engines developed some 400bhp, and were of the Brotherhood burner-cycle type. They were, in effect, semi-diesels using, traditionally, Shale oil as fuel with compressed air as the oxidant. On firing the torpedo, a spring loaded lever was released as it left the tube, and the engine started to turn by means of compressed air alone. After a pre-determined interval a mixture of fuel and air was ignited, by a percussion device, in a separate pre-heating chamber connected to the induction ring. This process did not seriously deplete the oxygen content of the air, and the hot gases passed to the cylinders through poppet valves. More fuel was injected just before piston top dead centre, at which point the unit became a more conventional, and highly efficient, engine. As the piston retracted, ports became exposed in the cylinder liner and the piston crown, and the products of combustion passed into the crankcase, into which water was sprayed for cooling and also as a diluent, and finally out through the hollow propeller shaft. In the mid 1930s a smaller 3.1 litre engine of the same type was put into production for the 18 inch (17.7 actual) Mk XI torpedo for airborne use, and for motor torpedo boats. Consequently, by 1935, the Admiralty contracts were becoming profitable for the company now that development work had been completed and achieved interchangeability of parts; this had been a major problem with these complicated engines, and indeed also with the gyroscopes.

A considerable number had been produced prior to the war, the 21 inch torpedo entering service in the 'O' Class submarines in about 1929, and the 18 inch in 1936. War production was to run to several thousands, and it is interesting to note that some of the later built Mk VIII torpedoes were still in service in 1983.

Agreement was reached with Coventry Corporation in December 1935 for the closure of Puma Road. Prior to this it had always been a public thoroughfare but, with the need for security in connection with military work, and the hazards involved in movements across the road, this was a sensible move. Also in December 1935, the engine names Deerhound and Terrier were registered. Of the former, more will be said in due course, whilst the latter has been suggested as being a 14 cylinder engine with Genet size cylinders, with a probable rating of around 250hp. However, the projected applications appear to indicate a much larger engine, and thus both configuration and size are suspect. A statement of note was made by Sopwith at the December Board meeting with respect to the importance of the large engines now under development, of which the Deerhound was one.

Fully restored, this elegant 1936 20-25hp Limousine is shown at the 1987 A.S.O.C. National Day. (*Author*)

Following John Siddeley's departure, the Board of Armstrong Siddeley Motors was reconstituted, and, in November 1936, Thomas Sopwith became chairman, whilst C.S. Oliver and the long term company secretary, A.J. Austen, were elected to the Board.

For 1936 the company offered five basic car models, the 12, 12 plus, 17 – in three chassis lengths – and the 20hp, with prices ranging from £285 to £745, and all with various body options, plus the Siddeley Special with a top price of £1,380. The 12 hp was now the only model with the old side valve engine, and even that was replaced during the year by a new overhead valve engine, which some outside critics regarded as yet another 'gutless' six, although bodywork was of the customary high standard. A new car was introduced during 1936, the 20 – 25hp, which was almost to assume the mantle of the Siddeley Special which was nearing the end of its production run. It featured a 3.7 litre engine capable of 85bhp, and could cope with almost two tons of bodywork, which it was often asked to carry in its limousine form. In its Atalanta sports saloon form, styled by Cyril Siddeley, it could comfortably top the 80mph mark. Among the many who were to favour this model were the Danish royal family and Neville Chamberlain, who was to become Prime Minister in 1937.

In general the bodywork was beginning to show a considerable softening of line, although remaining very upright in appearance, but were still superbly made, whether by the Burlington shop or the many outside coachbuilders, including the well known companies of Barkers, Holbrook, Hoyal, Maltby, Mulliner, Offord, Salmons and Vanden Plas. A new feature to be introduced was the Newton centrifugal clutch which, combined with the Wilson gearbox, contrived to make driving even smoother.

Of the aero engine range, only the Tiger, Cheetah, Lynx, and Panther remained, although a small number of the 7 cylinder Genet Major continued in production for the Cierva autogyros made by Avro. Main production now centred on the Tiger VIII, which, in 1936, became the world's first production engine with two speed supercharging, and also on the continually developing Cheetah.

Chassis for the 1937 20-25hp car.

A late thirties view of the Burlington body building shop, now part of the RB211/Development area.

The first production Whitley emerges from Baginton in 1937 powered by the 795hp Tiger IX. Wing dihedral was absent on early production aircraft but was retrospectively fitted. Below the starboard wing can be seen a Napier Dagger powered Hawker Hector. (*Imperial War Museum*).

The Tiger was now in demand for the Armstrong Whitworth Whitley, one of a trio of heavy bombers for the R.A.F., an engine contract to power 80 aircraft being received in August 1935. More Tigers were ordered in civil form for the largest pre-war British airliner the Armstrong Whitworth Ensign, a four engined aircraft originally ordered in September 1934. The Cheetah was now beginning its long production run for the Avro Anson, which had won a competition with the de Havilland Dragon Rapide for a communications aircraft and for use by Coastal Command. In July 1935 A.V. Roe had received an order for 174 of these aircraft, which was a service development of the Avro 652 civil aircraft, the first squadron receiving them in March 1936. Altogether almost a thousand aircraft were delivered prior to the war, and Parkside became hard pressed to cope with the demand.

Both of these engines featured an invention of the late 1920s by S.D. Heron, the ex-Parkside designer, in America. This was the sodium-cooled exhaust valve, which contributed greatly to carrying the heat of combustion away from the head of the valve to the stem and, like most other manufacturers, the company adopted it as quickly as possible. Sodium is extremely effective in transferring heat, but, as most who worked with it will verify, it was a horrible material to work with.

As recounted earlier, in 1935, development work began on a new 38.2 litre 21 cylinder engine to be known as the Deerhound. It was a three row engine, with seven banks of three in-line cylinders and overhead camshaft operated valves. The designed output was to be 1500hp for powering current and proposed heavy bomber projects. John Lloyd, Armstrong Whitworth Aircraft's Chief Designer, and the engine designers, would have preferred a water-cooled engine for the projected power output, but Siddeley would have none of it.

Ensign, the first of the AW.27's for Imperial Airways in 1938. Its Tiger engines were replaced during the war by Wright Cyclones. Note the massive undercarriage. All were impressed for war service, during which Ensign was badly damaged at Lagos in 1942 when the undercarriage was accidently retracted on the ground. (*R.A.F. Museum*).

This Anson GR MkI was powered by 350hp Cheetah IX engines and over 6,000 of the mark were produced. Armament consisted of a single .303 machine gun in the port side of the nose and a single Lewis gun in the dorsal turret. (*R.A.F. Museum*).

Designed in the mid 1930s the definitive version of the 38.2 litre 21 cylinder air-cooled Deerhound produced 1500hp on test. Note the between cylinder baffles for cooling the rear bank of cylinders.

The design was a direct descendant of the Hyena, and the experience with that engine was used to attempt adequate cooling for the rear row of cylinders by designing special air deflection passages between the cylinder banks. The engine was on test by the middle of 1938, but there were problems with the cylinders, which had to be redesigned, and testing was resumed in March 1939. Nine were built in total and the engine easily reached its designed output on the test bed within a comparatively short development time. Flight testing began with the original configuration of cylinders in January 1939 in a Whitley, but the aircraft crashed in March 1940 with fatal results for the aircrew. The crash was attributed to an incorrect tail trim setting, which had caused the aircraft to stall as it climbed away after take off. This unfortunate accident, although no fault of the engines, plus the old problem of cooling the rear bank of cylinders, for which a solution had now been found, caused the project to be shelved. However, work on the engine was restarted in 1940 when a Mk III version was designed with a slightly increased bore, but work on the first jet engine had begun by then and the project remained at the design stage. A forlorn reminder of the engine can be found in the series of photographs taken after one of the air raids showing one, still on its build stand, and apparently unharmed, surrounded by the wreckage of the development fitting shop.

Deerhound 21 cylinder radial engine installed in Armstrong Whitworth Whitley K.7243 in 1939.

Contemporaneously, a much larger engine was being designed called the Wolfhound. This may well be the oft alluded to 28 cylinder 4 row engine, probably with Deerhound size cylinders, but work on it was discontinued following the problems with the Deerhound. An even larger 66.5 litre 27 cylinder engine, the Boarhound, was also designed prior to the war. The provisional specification for the engine quotes a maximum power output of 2,300hp at 2,700rpm, which appears very conservative. Once again, it was a 3 row engine, with nine banks of 3 in-line cylinders, and had a maximum diameter of only 51 inches, the same as the Tiger engine. However, with the proximity of war, and the problems already encountered with the Deerhound, it did not progress beyond the design stage, although there is some evidence that some single cylinder development may have commenced.

Considerably more orders were to arrive at Parkside following the adoption of the Airspeed Oxford as the R.A.F.'s advanced training aircraft. It first flew in June 1937 powered by a Cheetah IX, but went into squadron service in November with the 340hp direct drive Cheetah X. The initial production order was for 350 aircraft, and several training squadrons had been equipped with them prior to the war: ultimately some 8,000 were produced. Armstrong Siddeley had earlier associations with Airspeed, having previously powered their Courier, Envoy and the Queen Wasp target aircraft.

By the middle of 1938, Cheetah production was running at some 20 – 25 per week and was expected to reach 30 by December. The maximum capacity of the factory was stated to be 40, and above that the company would have to resort to sub-contracting.

The cowled Deerhound in Whitley K7243, 1939. The large scoop below the engine was for cooling air to the rear of the engine, replacing an earlier installation using an extra long chord circular cowling. The war, and the Whitley crash, halted development.

Having almost finished production of the Tiger, the company was somewhat dismayed by the receipt of a further order for 50 in October, which entailed a considerable amount of re-organisation in order to maintain the Cheetah production.

From the mid 1930s there had been a marked deterioration in the political situation in Europe, due to the aspirations of the German Chancellor, Adolf Hitler, and in September 1938, Neville Chamberlain flew to Munich to meet Hitler. The government's policy was one of appeasement, and Chamberlain arrived back with the famous 'peace in our time' document. Whilst it convinced the majority of the population, it did nothing to curb the rapid increase in rearmament. This was to result in an increase in the production of self-changing boxes at Parkside for the new armoured vehicles in 1939. However, in 1938 the last military vehicle in which Parkside had a direct involvement had appeared. This was in the form of an armoured car for the R.A.F. on a Siddeley 6 x 4 chassis (6 wheels with 4 wheels driven). Despite the fact that this car is well illustrated, there is virtually nothing known about it, either of its specification or exactly where it was built. The configuration was thoroughly modern, but the design has no affinity to any other company's vehicles. Its purpose appears to have been for airfield defence only, and not for work over rough ground, since the rear axles had single wheels only, with tyres similar to normal commercial vehicles. It was powered by a rear mounted air-cooled V8 engine, whose power output is at present unknown, and was armed with a single, turret-mounted, .303 Vickers machine gun.

The aftermath of the Deerhound Whitley crash in March 1940 caused by elevator trim tab problems. Engine remains can be seen beyond the fuselage, centre. The crew, unfortunately, lost their lives.

For the 1938 Motor Show, two completely new cars were on show, one of which was a 2 litre 16hp model shown in saloon form only. In its cheapest form it was still excellent value at £380, but there were signs of utility with the fitting of white faced instruments, as fitted to many cheaper cars, a narrower radiator grille and, although the Sphinx mascot was retained, the previous screw-in cap was replaced and the Sphinx swung up like a cigarette box lid to reveal the radiator filler cap. The engine was a completely new design with overhead valves, and was to form the basis for the post-war car engines.

The remainder of the range were also featured, the 14, 17, 20 and 25hp all having minor differences in styling and features, but the Siddeley Special had now disappeared. They ranged in price from £335 for the basic 14hp, up to £745 for the luxury 25hp. The year also saw the end of the old style disc wheels, all models featuring pressed steel ones with attachment closer to the hub centre. For 1939 the company decided to manufacture only the saloon bodies at Parkside, all other body forms being supplied from outside builders.

A completely new 20hp model called the Ensign was also shown in 1938, but was dropped early the following year as a policy decision, probably due to the worsening situation in Europe. This model was fitted with independent front suspension at Sopwith's suggestion, and also featured a completely new engine which delivered 85bhp from a modest 2.8 litre capacity.

Parkside's reputation for versatility was to be further put to the test in 1938 after the company entered the machine tool field. The Coventry firm of A.C.Wickman had

The aircraft which marked the real beginning of the King's (now Queen's) flight was this Cheetah IX powered Envoy III delivered in 1937 for the transport of 'Royalty and State personages'. Following war service it returned to civilian use and was one of only two Envoys to fly after the war. (*British Aerospace*).

received a large order from Russia for their Wickman Moulton thread milling machines, but the required delivery date was beyond their capacity. One hundred of these machines were subcontracted to Parkside and a production facility was set up in the Middle Machine Shop. The completion date was scheduled for November, but it is doubtful if this was achieved, nor indeed whether the entire contract was ever completed. Unfortunately it was not to be a lucrative one, and it was reported to the Board that a loss of £3,000 was expected.

Management changes were a prominent factor in 1939, beginning with the announcement in February of the resignation of Lt. Col. L.F.R. Fell from both the Board and his position of Chief Engineer (Aero Engines). Fell was a highly respected engineer who had held the post of Assistant Director of the Directorate of Technical Development – Engines in 1921. In 1927 he resigned the post and joined Rolls-Royce, along with J.E. Ellor of supercharger fame, following several dealings with Henry Royce on new engine designs. He moved to Parkside in March 1934 and was elected to the Board in March 1935.

In July 1939, Thomas Sopwith resigned in order to concentrate on the Hawker Siddeley side of the business and was succeeded by F.S. Spriggs (later Sir Frank) who had joined the Armstrong Siddeley Board in 1935 along with Sopwith. H.K. Jones, who had joined the Board in 1937, became Managing Director whilst C.S. Oliver remained as General Manager. At some time during the year H.T. Chapman had been promoted from Production Manager to the post of Works Manager.

Used in the Airspeed Oxford the Cheetah X was a medium supercharged engine with direct drive to the fixed pitch wooden propeller. With an international rating of 340hp at 2,300rpm this engine, together with the Mk IX, began the prolific output of Cheetahs throughout the war.

As the European situation continued to deteriorate, Oliver asked the Board to consider spending the sum of £30,000 on the provision of protection for the workforce if war was declared, with the inevitable risk of air raids. The Board agreed to the proposal providing government approval was forthcoming. It was also stated that there

Powered by the 295hp Cheetah X engine the Airspeed A.S.10 Oxford Mk 1 was built in considerable numbers, both before and throughout the war. The aircraft illustrated are from 3 Flying Training School, based at South Cerney, about 1938.

Armoured car for R.A.F. airfield defence c1937 on a Parkside 6 x 4 chassis with rear mounted air-cooled engine. Its specification is unknown, neither is it known if the bodywork was built here. (*The Tank Museum*)

Styled by Cyril Siddeley, the Atalanta body was available on most chassis. Here it is carried by the 1938 model 20/25hp at Sutton Park.

A 1938 25hp Town and Country Saloon in sylvan surroundings.

In showroom condition, this 1938 17hp Limousine carried a price of £585.

The 1939 16hp Coach Saloon at Charlecote Park.

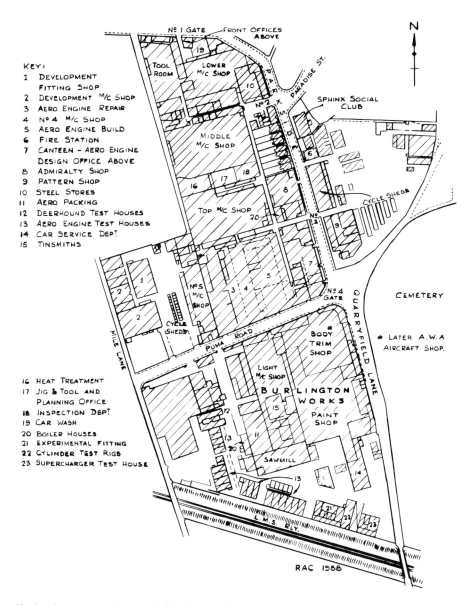

No site plans appear to have survived for the period immediately prior to the war, and this map has been compiled from the only known print of the bomb damage sustained at Parkside; the negative of which appears not to have survived. The original can be dated between September 1939, when car production ceased, and April 1941, when the Development area was destroyed.

Scheduled to be introduced for 1939 the 20hp Ensign Coach Saloon featured independent front suspension for the first time at Parkside. However, it was decided that it should not go into production.

would be no money available for car production and that the factory would be engaged solely on government work. Meanwhile, the new 16hp was exceeding its sales target with some 500 sold before March and another 500 on build. Sales were confidently expected to exceed 30 per week. The company was also considering a new 12hp model, but this was in its very early design stage, although prototypes had been sanctioned.

Production of the Cheetah continued to increase and had reached 40 per week, with a further 8 or 9 per week coming off the repair line. It was expected to reach a target of 60 per week by June, providing subcontracting was satisfactory, with repairs rising to 20 per week. The Cheetah XI was now ready for production, being the first geared version and rated at 460hp. The complications with the new order for the Tiger having been resolved, it was stated that production would commence in May if all went well.

A further contract had been secured by the company at some time in 1938, from the North Eastern Marine Engineering Company, for ten of a new type of diesel engine to be called the Nemesis. The first of these sombrely named engines was completed early in 1939, and was stated to be a first class unit and was running well. As with several other engines, few details of it are known other than that it was a 4 cylinder inline engine for commercial vehicles, but production was to begin on the remainder of the contract, although the pressure of war resulted in the final one not being produced until 1943/4.

Production of the Wilson gearbox for tanks had continued at a comparatively steady rate over the last few years but, with the current influx of Cheetah work, the decision was taken in 1938 to utilise Parkside as an assembly facility only, all parts for the boxes being manufactured by subcontractors. Large contracts had been placed in 1938 for the new A12 Matilda infantry tank, which was due to enter service the following year, and Parkside received the contract for the Wilson gearboxes. The Matilda had been designed by the Mechanisation Board at Woolwich and was derived from the experimental A7 tanks of 1932, although it was not really suitable for mass production.

Although photographed in 1942 this is basically the 1939 4 light 16hp Touring Saloon. Of interest are the headlamp covers which gave a shaded slit beam of light to conform to wartime blackout regulations.

The gearbox was part of a transmission line of a non-regenerative system used in all tanks prior to 1940. In effect, this meant that, for steering, the lower power required by the inner track could not be transferred to boost that of the outer one, and in consequence, the full power output was not available for traction when it was most needed in order to maintain speed while traversing difficult terrain. The basic transverse drive from the gearbox could be of two types: the clutch and brake type, which required heavy and massive components, or with the drive system improved by the insertion of a multi-ratio epicyclic gearbox in each half shaft. This latter system is known as geared steering, and whilst it allowed a certain amount of power transfer, it also made the system even heavier and more complex. The Matilda was equipped with the latter and, despite its many shortcomings, was the only British tank to remain in service throughout the war, albeit in several guises.

Chamberlain's policy of appeasement was now in tatters as Hitler's expansionist policies were put into action. In March 1938 he annexed Austria, and in September, the Sudetenland – part of Czechoslovakia, but with a largely ethnic German population – following political control passing to the Nazis in the region. During March 1939 he completed the annexation of the formerly German part of the country, Bohemia and Moravia, after coercing the Czech government into abdicating the sovereignty of the regions. He next turned his attentions on Poland and demanded the return of the free port of Danzig to German control. This was Poland's only outlet to the sea and they refused. Negotiations dragged on, Hitler demanding concession and, following Munich, thinking that the pacifist governments of both Britain and France would not dare to honour agreements with Poland. The result was inevitable, and Germany invaded Poland on 1 September 1939, but his gamble failed, and both Britain and France declared war on 3 September 1939.

Lest we forget. The war changed the face of old Coventry for ever. This 1935 photograph from the roof above the Reception Area near No. 1 Gate shows the former magnificence of the Cathedral of St Michael. Still extant, and just visible bottom left, is the Greyhound pub in Much Park Street.

The general mobilisation which was ordered on 1 September took many men from Parkside to the war; however, some who volunteered were told that their services were more essential to the plant than to the services. Car production abruptly ceased as all resources were turned to the war effort; the dark years of deprivation, long and uncertain hours, and personal tragedies had begun.

APPENDIX I

The aero engines:

Engines attaining production status:

Name	Type	Introduced	Bore	Stroke	Capacity (litres)	Power Range
Puma	6cyl water-cooled Inline	1918	145mm	190mm	18.8	246hp
Tiger	12cyl water-cooled Vee Inline	1919	160mm	180mm	43.5	500–650hp
Jaguar (original)	14cyl 2 Row air-cooled Radial	1920	5.0"	5.0"	22.4	300hp
Jaguar (later)		1923	5.0"	5.5"	24.8	360–470hp
Ounce	2cyl Horizontally Opposed air-cooled	1920	5.0"	5.0"	3.2	45hp
Lynx	7cyl air-cooled Radial	1925	5.0"	5.5"	12.4	180–215hp
Genet	5cyl air-cooled Radial	1926	4.0"	4.0"	4.1	60–80hp
Mongoose	5cyl air-cooled Radial	1926	5.0"	5.5"	8.9	150hp
Leopard	14cyl 2 Row air-cooled Radial	1928	6.0"	7.5"	48.6	700–805hp
Genet Major	5cyl air-cooled Radial	1929	4.25"	4.5"	5.2	100hp
Jaguar Major —later Panther	14cyl 2 Row air-cooled Radial	1929	5.25"	5.5"	27.3	600–750hp
Lynx Major —later Cheetah	7cyl air-cooled Radial	1929	5.25"	5.5"	13.65	260–400hp
(Cheetah XI)	7cyl air-cooled Radial	1939	5.25"	5.0"	12.42	415hp
Double Mongoose —later Serval	10cyl 2 Row air-cooled Radial	1930/1	5.0"	5.5"	17.7	300–380hp
Genet Major —later Civet	7cyl air-cooled Radial	1931	4.25"	4.5"	7.3	143–160hp

128

Name	Type	Introduced	Bore	Stroke	Capacity (litres)	Power Range
Tiger	14cyl 2 Row air-cooled Radial	1932	5.5"	6.0"	32.7	720–840hp

APPENDIX II

Engines built for development, or as prototypes:

Name	Type	Introduced	Bore	Stroke	Capacity (litres)	Power Range
C I Engine (Diesel)	14cyl 2 Row air-cooled Radial	about 1930	6.375"	7.75"	56.75	650hp
Mastiff	14cyl 2 Row air-cooled Radial	about 1932		No Details Known		
Hyena	15cyl 3 Row air-cooled Radial – Cylinder Rows In Line	1933	137mm	125mm	26.6	618hp
Deerhound	21cyl 3 Row air-cooled Radial – Cylinder Rows In Line	1935	135mm	127mm	38.2	1500hp (on test)
Deerhound Mk III	21cyl 3 Row air-cooled Radial – Cylinder Rows In Line	1940	140mm	127mm	41.05	Not Known

Engines projected or at design stage only:

Name	Type	Introduced	Bore	Stroke	Capacity (litres)	Power Range
Wolfhound	Configuration very uncertain	about 1936		No Details Known		
Boarhound	27cyl 3 Row air-cooled Radial – Cylinder Rows In Line	1936/7	140mm	160mm	66.5	2300 hp (estimated)
Terrier	14cyl 2 Row air-cooled Radial	1935		No Details – Those at present suggested are very suspect given the projected applications.		
Whippet	Configuration unknown	about 1935		No Details Known		

APPENDIX III

The Cars:

Model	Intro	Cyls	Valves	Bore mm	Stroke mm	Capacity (cc)	Notes
30hp	1919	6	OHV	88.9	133.4	4960	Vee Honeycomb Radiator
18hp	1921	6	OHV	69.5	104.8	2318	Vee Honeycomb Radiator
4/14hp	1923	4	OHV	76.2	101.6	1852	Flat Honeycomb Radiator
30hp Mk II	1925	6	OHV	88.9	133.4	4960	Vee Honeycomb Radiator
18hp Mk II	1925	6	OHV	69.5	104.8	2318	Vee Honeycomb Radiator
4/14hp Mk II	1925	4	OHV	76.2	101.6	1852	Flat Honeycomb Radiator
15hp	1927	6	SV	63.5	101	1900	Flat Honeycomb Radiator
(New Engine)	1932	6	SV	63.5	114	2169	Vee Honeycomb Radiator 1930 – Vee Shell With Flat Radiator 1931
20hp	1927	6	OHV	73	114.2	2872	Vee Honeycomb Radiator
(New Engine)	1932	6	OHV	73	127	3190	Known as 'New 20' – Vee Shell With Flat Radiator Core
12hp	1928	6	OHV	56	84	1236	Flat Honeycomb Radiator
Became: New 12hp	1931	6	SV	59.25	84	1434	Vee Shell With Flat Radiator
Became: 12+	1935	6	OHV	61	95.25	1666	– all had this feature from this point*
Siddeley Special	1932	6	OHV	88.9	133.4	4960	
17hp	1934	6	OHV	66.6	114	2394	
Siddeley Special Mk II	1935			Engine Details as 1932 Mk I			

Model	Intro	Cyls	Valves	Bore mm	Stroke mm	Capacity (cc)	Notes
14hp	1936	6	OHV	61	95.25	1666	
20/25hp	1937	6	OHV	82.5	114	3670	Known as 25hp in 1938
16hp	1939	6	OHV	65	100	1990	Vee shell less pronounced

Prototypes Only:

Model	Intro	Cyls	Valves	Bore mm	Stroke mm	Capacity (cc)	Notes
20hp	1939	6	OHV	75	105	2780	Vee shell with flat radiator

Featured independent front suspension – only 'Ensign' Coach Saloon thought to have been built.

Details:

*With the exception of the Economy 12hp which, whilst featuring a slatted shell, merely hinted at the Vee form by being slightly curved. It carried the full Vee form in 1932.

Seated Sphinx replaced by prone Sphinx for 1932 – Louvred bonnet sides replaced by more modern horizontal pattern in 1938.

APPENDIX IV

Other Armstrong Siddeley Designed Engines

Tank Engines:

Engine: 6 cyl water-cooled Puma – See APPENDIX 1

Used In: Experimental Medium D Tank 1920
- Length: 30 ft
- Width (over tracks): 7 ft 5 in
- Height: 9 ft 2 in
- Weight: 20 tons
- Crew: 3
- Speed: 23mph
- Armament: 3 Machine Guns
- Armour: 8 – 10 mm

Engine: 90hp V8 air-cooled OHV
- Bore: 4.0"
- Stroke: 4.75"
- Capacity: 7.79 litres
- Weight: 1022 lbs
- Power Output: 90bhp at 1600rpm

Used In:
- 1923 Armstrong Siddeley built horn-steering Dragon designation: B1E1 – No details known
- 1924 Vickers Medium Mk I Tank 11.7 tons – one 3pdr gun and 4 Hotchkiss and 2 Vickers .303 machine guns – 6.5mm armour – 17' 6" long x 9'1" wide – 15mph
- 1925 Vickers Medium Mk II Tank 13.2 tons – armament as above – 8.25mm armour – 17' 6" long x 9' 1" wide – 15mph.
Details of Dragons based on the Medium tank not known.
- 1926 Birch Gun: 18pdr field gun on Vickers designed tracked vehicle – no other details known
- 1928 Vickers Wheel and Track Tank D3E1: 8.4 tons – 2 Vickers .303 machine guns – 18' long x 8' wide – 15mph on tracks, 45mph on wheels (with tracked running gear retracted).

Engine: 30hp 6 cylinder water-cooled – probably a modified Siddeley Six car engine.

Used In: 1924 Small Dragon B1E2 – designed and built at Parkside – 3 tons – 12mph on road, 8mph across country – 8 crew.

Engine: 60hp V4 air-cooled – no details known

Used In: 1925 Light dragon B1E3. Engine, transmission and chassis possibly designed and built at Parkside. Bodywork definitely by Armstrong Whitworth at Newcastle-upon-Tyne.

Engine:	375hp V12 air-cooled OHV
	Bore: 5.75" Weight: Not quoted
	Stroke: 7.0" Power Output: 350bhp at 1500rpm
	Capacity: 35.8 litres Cost: £27,500 (quotation)
	Comp Ratio: 4.7 to 1
Used In:	Vickers Armstrong Heavy Tank A1E1 Independent. 31.5 tons – one 3pdr gun and 4 Vickers .303 machine guns. 13-28 mm Armour – 25' 5" long x 10' 6" wide – 25mph road speed
Engine:	45hp 4 Cylinder air-cooled – a 4 cylinder version of Medium Mk I engine.
Used In:	Armstrong Siddeley built Pavesi 4 wheel (solid tyred) tractors, 4 wheel (pneumatic-tyred – 40" x 9") reconnaissance car and 8wheel (pneumatic tyred) tractor. *NOTE* A second 8 wheel Pavesi used a Genet aero engine – See Appendix 1.
Engine:	180hp at 1800rpm V8 air-cooled – No details known
Used In:	1928 2 experimental A6 Vickers Armstrong Tanks (16 tonner). 17.5 tons – one 3pdr gun and 5 Vickers .303 machine guns – 9-14 mm Armour – 21'6" long x 8'9" wide – 30 mph
	1930 Vickers Medium Mk III tank 16 tons – one 3pdr gun and 3 Vickers .303 machine guns – 9-14mm Armour – 21'6" long x 8'10" wide – 30mph
Engine:	120hp V8 air-cooled – No details known
Used In:	1930 2 experimental A7 tanks built by Royal Ordnance Factory.14 tons – one 3pdr gun and 2 Vickers .303 machine guns – 9-14 mm Armour – 22'6" long x 8'11" wide – 25 mph
Engine:	87bhp 4 cylinder air-cooled – No details known
Used In:	Vickers 6 ton Mk E 'A' and 'B' tanks. 8 tons – 5/8/14mm Armour 15'0" long x 7'11" wide – 22mph
Engine:	25hp 2 cylinder air-cooled – probably horizontally opposed, and using 2 Medium Mk.I engine cylinders.
Used In:	1930 Carden-Loyd Mk VIa tankettes. 1 ton 18 cwt – 1 Vickers .303 machine gun – 9mm armour – 8' 1" long x 5' 7" wide – speed about 30mph – 2 crew.

Torpedo Engines:

Type:	4 cylinder radial burner-cycle (semi-diesel) engine with air pre-heating chamber in induction ring
Designer:	Peter Brotherhood of Peter Brotherhood & Co., Peterborough
Fuel:	Broxburn Lighthouse Shale Oil (5 other brands of commercial kerosene were also suitable)
Oxidant:	Compressed Air

Ignition: Twin percussion igniters

Valves: One poppet valve, for pre-heated air, and one fuel injection nozzle per cylinder.

Cooling: by internal saltwater (seawater) spray to crankcase

Engine for Mk VIII Series 21" Torpedoes   Introduced 1927

Bore: 4.5"
Stroke: 4.4"
Capacity: 4.59 litres

Fuel Capacity: 30lbs
Air Capacity: 15.64 cu ft at 2500 psi
Range: 5000 yards at 45.5 knots
      7000 yards at 41 knots

Comp Ratio: about 20 to 1
Power Output:
Nom: 320 bhp at 1200rpm (1939)

Weight: 210 lbs

Engine for Mk XI (XII) 45cm (17.7") Torpedoes   Introduced 1936 (1937)

Bore: 4.0"
Stroke: 3.75"
Capacity: 3.08 litres

Fuel Capacity: 7.5lbs   (Mk XII)
Air Capacity: 6.45 cu ft at 1600 psi (Mk XII)
Range: 1500 yards at 40 knots
      3000 yards at 27 knots
      (1500 yards at 40 knots)
      (3500 yards at 27 knots)

Comp Ratio: –

Power Output:
Max: 225bhp at 1230 rpm
(Later 270bhp at 1340 rpm)

Weight: 120 lbs

Figures in parentheses are those for Mk XII Torpedo

Railcar Details:

Length: 54' 9¾"
Width: 8' 8"
Height: 11' 2"
Weight: 10½ tons in running order

Speed: 70mph
Tyres: Special 35.25" dia Michelin Pneumatic with integral puncture sensors.
90 – 100 psi pressure

Engine: 275hp V12 water-cooled (design based on Siddeley Special engine)

Bore: 4.0"
Stroke: 5.25"
Capacity: 13 litres

Valves: OHV – exhaust valve sodium-cooled
Weight: 981 lbs dry
Power Output: 275bhp at 3000rpm

Details: Hiduminium crankcase, cylinder block and head, with wet liners. Forged Hiduminium connecting rods and pistons. Hydraulic pushrods.
4 speed Wilson epicyclic gearbox for forward and reverse running.

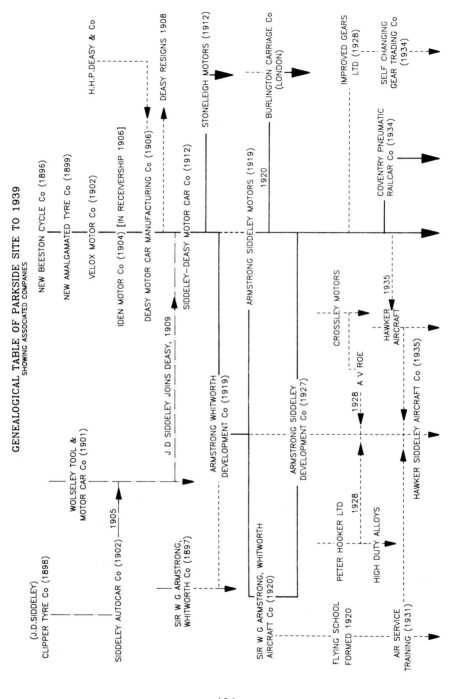

APPENDIX VI

Historical details of other companies connected with the story of Parkside:

Calcott Brothers Limited:

This company began life in 1896 as one of the many cycle manufacturers in Coventry, and the facade of their former premises in Far Gosford Street is still extant. They did not produce their first car until 1913, and generally tended to concentrate on the light car market. Altogether they produced some 2,500 cars before being acquired by the Singer company in 1926.

Charlesworth Bodies Works:

Founded in 1908 by Messrs. Hill, Steane and Gray, this company had a chequered history in the manufacture of car bodies: the first bodies for both Calcott and Hillman being manufactured there. Their speciality was the cabriolet, and they held more patents for folding hoods and seats than any other company. Mass production techniques were never introduced, and at one time they were said to be the only body-builders outside London still producing hand built bodies. Output was about 10 per week and they also produced tailor-made bodies; one of the most famous being one for an invalid lady where a seat moved to the rear of the car at the touch of a button, through a central door in the back of the car, from where the mechanism lowered the chair to the ground. A photograph exists of an Armstrong Siddeley advertisement with a similar arrangement, and this may well be the same vehicle.

Much development work on airframes was carried out for Siddeley-Deasy during World War 1, and John Lloyd had an office there when he first moved to Parkside from the Royal Aircraft Factory at Farnborough.

Reconstituted in 1931, the company appears to have ceased trading after being severely damaged in the Coventry blitz in 1940.

Humber Cycle Company:

The original lessees of the Parkside site in 1896 had associations with the Humber, formed in 1875 by Thomas Humber and Thomas Marriott in Nottingham. The company already had a cycle factory here by 1890, but their entire operation moved to Coventry from its later premises in Beeston, a suburb of Nottingham, in 1908. As a motor company, Humber had been building cars under licence since 1896, but following the acquistion of property in Humber Road – its present name – in Coventry, all car production was also transferred here. Moving into the field of aero-engine manufacture in 1909, and into aircraft in 1910, they contributed much to the war effort in both

World Wars. Essentially motor manufacturers, they were taken over by the Rootes Group in 1930.

Iden Motor Car Company:

This company was set up by George Iden, formerly the Works Manager at the Motor Manufacturing Company in Coventry, in premises vacated by Velox (q.v.). Its first cars were 4 cylinder 12hp and 18hp models with shaft drive.

A 25hp was introduced for 1905, but was only made for that season, although the other two models continued. The company was in receivership early in 1906, but, nevertheless, moved to premises in Fleet Street in Coventry. The final model was a 12hp V-twin with front wheel drive, and appears to have been built in what must have been considerably smaller premises. It was intended primarily for taxicab work, but was not made in quantity. George Iden's later history is not known after the company went out of business in 1907.

Maudslay Motor Company:

Formed in 1902 by a member of the Maudslay family, Cyril C. Maudslay; the parent company being the world renowned marine engine makers. Their initial models were designed by Alexander Craig, later to move to Calcotts, and quickly established a reputation for easy maintenance, safety and longevity. Their cars were early in the field with overhead camshafts, more for serviceability than for power, and were almost always in the higher powered range from around 25hp to 60hp. During the first World War most of their production was in the field of commercial vehicles, and it was this aspect of the company's business which brought about the cessation of car production in 1926. The company was finally absorbed into the A.E.C. group in 1951, the Parkside premises being vacated in 1953.

Rover Car Company:

This company began life as the Rover Cycle Company in the 1880s. One of its most famous employees was J.K.Starley, the accepted father of the bicycle we know today. Their first essay into car production was in 1904 with an 8hp single cylinder model which featured a tubular chassis. The well known shield shaped radiator was introduced in 1907, and this was still recognisable until about 1949. The company had three premises in Coventry, and also had an interest in the Parkside Motor Body Works which were sandwiched between the Armstrong Siddeley and Maudslay works, fronting onto Parkside. Many famous cars emerged from this stable, but in 1948 the company moved to Solihull, near Birmingham, and were finally merged with Leyland in 1966.

Standard Motor Company:

Formed in 1903 by another of the Maudslay family, R.W.Maudslay, its first car was an under-floor engined single cylinder model. Their famous Union Jack badge appeared in 1908, and featured on most models until the end of their separate existence. In the early years, the company's reputation was built up by offering relatively inexpensive large 6 cylinder cars. After suffering badly in the recession of the 1920s, the company gained a new Managing Director, Captain John Black, in 1929 and it gradually resumed its place among the major car manufacturers. Perhaps best known for its 'Flying' series of cars in the 1930s, it was one of the first to introduce a new model after the war with the Vanguard. During World War 2 they are best remembered as a builder of many dH Mosquito aircraft and consequently, received many enemy visitations – with, fortunately, little success. Also during the war the company used part of the site at Ansty for the manufacture and the storage of airframes. After the war we, in turn, used the motor company's facilities for testing of Viper engines when demand outstripped the internal capacity. After acquiring the Triumph Motor Car Company in 1945, they were swallowed up by the expanding Leyland company in 1960.

Swift of Coventry:

Unique in the annals of the transport history of Coventry, the old established Coventry Sewing Machine Company brought the cycle-making trade to the city when, in 1865, Josiah Turner was persuaded by his nephew to manufacture 400 early cycles.

In order to fulfil this, the company name was changed to the Coventry Machinists Company, and eventually became Swift of Coventry in 1919. Car manufacture began in 1898, but serious production did not commence until a new factory was opened in 1906, divorced by some 200 yards from the cycle factory. It is probable that this factory was next door to the chocolate factory in Mile Lane, but by 1919 the company held considerably more of the land fronting Mile Lane.

Their cars were highly regarded, and won several honours in the period 1904 – 1906; in the latter year winning a Gold Medal in the Scottish Reliability Trial. The very popular cyclecar appeared in 1912, and over the years the company's name was synonymous with rugged simplicity. However, by the late 1920s they were feeling the intense competition of the mass production makers, such as Austin and Morris, and finally ceased to trade in 1931.

Velox Motor Company:

This company was set up in 1902 in the area opposite Short Street – now the front offices – under a lease from the New Amalgamated Tyre Company, although details of the lease are at present unknown. Their first model was a 10hp car with a two cylinder Abeille engine, with shaft drive to the rear axle. Two models were made in 1903, a 10hp with a 4 cylinder Forman engine, and the Miniature Velox, a two seater with a single cylinder 4hp Aster engine – both featuring shaft drive. Although adding a 20hp car to the range in 1903, the company was, by then, in the process of being wound up, which finally occurred during 1904. Only 21 cars were made in all.